Beastly Buildings

Walter Ford's 'Ideal Kennel' (1874)

THE NATIONAL TRUST BOOK OF
ARCHITECTURE FOR ANIMALS

Beastly
Buildings

Lucinda Lambton

THE ATLANTIC MONTHLY PRESS
BOSTON/NEW YORK

First American Edition

85-73156

Printed in Italy

Contents

Acknowledgements

For permission to use copyright material, I would like to thank Her Majesty the Queen (the dairy, aviary and poultry-house at Windsor), the Royal Pavilion, Art Gallery and Museums, Brighton (Porden's stables), the Trustees of the British Museum (Rossetti's wombat), Dr Eva Crane (the castle for bees at Berthddu), the Royal Institute of British Architects (the fishing temple at Virginia Water; the gibbon-house at London Zoo), Mary Evans Picture Library (the ideal kennel), the Trustees of Sir John Soane's Museum (the canine residences; the nesting-boxes at Wimpole), the Marquis of Tavistock and Trustees of the Woburn Estates (Woburn dairy, aviary and the temple to Che Foo) and the Zoological Society of London (the monkey-house at London Zoo).

I would also like to thank the following for their great help, kindness, guidance and tolerance, always laced with good humour: Mr G. Adams, Mr and Mrs L. G. Allgood, Ian Anstruther, Rene Baker, Lt-Colonel H. H. Barneby, the Duke and Duchess of Beaufort, the Duke and Duchess of Bedford, Charles Beresford-Clark, Mr J. Berkeley, Mrs Margaret Biggs, Simon Blow, Mr H. Bonfield, Sir William and Lady Boulton, Tony Brainsby, British Telecom (Wotton, Surrey), Mr and Mrs R. Brooks, John Bull, Mr and Mrs R. Caffyn, Mr H. R. M. Calder, Richard Carew-Pole, The Lady Anne Cavendish-Bentinck, the Dowager Marchioness Cholmondeley, Sir John and Lady Clerk of Penicuik, Mr and Mrs Clifford, the Hon. L. H. L. Cohen, Patrick Connor, M. B: Cook, Mrs B. Cooke, Julian Cooksey, Mr A. Cooper, Mr A. T. P. Cooper, Mr and Mrs C. Cottrell-Dormer, Mr T. Cottrell-Dormer, Mr J. S. Cox, Commander Crawford, Mrs Ann Crookshank, Mr D. Crowden, Mr and Mrs Dalrymple, Gillian Darley, Sir Francis Dashwood, Mr M. Davis, Warren Davis, the Duchess of Devonshire, Jill Dew, Miss Margaret Dickinson, Alan Dodd, Richard Downing, Captain Humphrey and the Hon. Mrs Drummond, The Lady Dulverton, the Bishop of Durham, Mr R. Earle, Jill Edwards, Lord Eliot, Mr N. E. Elliott, Dr A. W. Exell, Edmund Fairfax-Lucy, Mr and Mrs B. Feilding, Mr Roger Fleetwood-Hesketh and Lady Mary Hesketh, Mr and Mrs Fretwell, the Earl and Countess of Gainsborough, Mr B. J. Gibbs, Mrs Pamela Gilbert, Mr Timothy Gilbert, Mark Girouard, the Knight of Glin and Madame Fitzgerald, the Gloucestershire College of Agriculture, Sir Charles Graham, Francis Graham, Miss R. Griffin, Desmond and Penny Guinness, Mr I. Hadgkiss, the Harpur-Crewe Estate, John and Eileen Harris, Lady Harrod, Barnaby and Huckleberry Harrod, the Hon. Lady Hastings, Lord Hastings, Mr and Mrs J. Hegarty, Christian Lady Hesketh, Lord and Lady Hesketh, Mr F. Hetherington, Myles Hildyard, the Historic Buildings and Monuments Directorate (Scotland), Mr and Mrs G. Holbech, Mr and Mrs D. W. Houlston, Mr and Mrs J. Howard, Neil Hynd, Mary Innes, Ian Irvine, Gervaise Jackson-Stops, Mr and Mrs S. Jacques, Derek Keen, Mr D. Keyte, Lord and Lady Lambton, Arabella Lennox-Boyd, the London Library, the Earl and Countess of Lichfield, the Marquis of Londonderry, Mr P. McKay, Deirdre Mackinnon, Mr and Mrs B. Martin, Mr G. Miller, Sir John Miller, Miss E. Mills, Sir John Musker, Rose Musker, Mr M. Newman, Isabella and Phillip Neylor-Leyland, Mrs D. Norman, City of Nottingham Museums, Lawrence Oates, Adrian Palmer, the Earl of Pembroke, Mrs P. M. Price, John Martin Robinson, David Rowbotham, the Duke and Duchess of Rutland, Mr R. Scott, Mr J. T. Sharp, Mrs P. Sharratt, Mr and Mrs Slater, Mr and Mrs Spenser, Stephen and Clare Squarey, Staffordshire County Council, Mr and Mrs Freddie Stockdale, the Duke of Sutherland, Sir Tatton Sykes, Mr and Mrs Taylor, Mr M. Tebbutt, Mr and Mrs Thomson, Colonel R. Waller, Major A. J. Warre, Lavinia Wellecombe, the Duke of Wellington, the Duke and Duchess of Westminster, the Earl of Weymss, Mr and Mrs S. C. Whitbread, Mrs June Williams, Mr and Mrs Kit Williams, Jack Willoughby, Sir Marcus and Lady Worsley, Mr R. K. Wynn, the Earl and Countess of Yarborough, Mrs David Young.

Introduction

John Bunyan said that an Englishman would rather walk with a dog than with a fellow Christian. It is the same today: British reserve is abandoned when faced with a dog, cat or budgerigar, and the most stoically unemotional will find they possess a sentimental streak. Animals have provided an excuse to build fantastic structures, and on the foundation of eccentricity and extravagance, fashion and immense fortunes, a quantity of remarkable houses for animals have risen up all over the country. The inhabitants could never complain, however idiosyncratic their dwelling, and the builder's imagination could flourish unbridled, often unconstrained by architectural convention. An obelisk to a pig, a tomb to a trout, a pyramid for poultry, a temple for terrapins and castles for bears, salmon, bees, deer, hounds, doves and cows – all provided an enjoyable outlet for the wildest flights of architectural fancy. This book is my tribute to these two passions, the delight in animals and the architecture that honours it.

I have tried to impose some sort of order on a multitude of oddities by dividing the book into four sections: Sport, the Stomach, Decoration, and Death.

'Sport' produced the grandest architecture, giving us great shrines to bear-, bull- and badger-baiting, to cock-fighting, to fishing, shooting, coursing and racing, and to the hunting of stag, hare and fox.

Deer-hunting was common until well into the eighteenth century, and it still goes on today. In the nineteenth century, the wretched creatures were victims of the practice of 'carting'. Tamed and trained, they would be delivered to the waiting hunt in a cart, and then pursued more for the chase than for the kill, a meagre consolation for the creature with a dislocated hip or a tendon cut to make it an easier quarry. A stag that was taken too 'quik' by Elizabeth I in 1575 was granted his life in exchange for the ransom of 'hiz earz', and in 1793 a report of a hunt records that a stag was pursued for four and a half hours before he dropped dead at the end of a run at Marlow. There was a fine crop of buildings – houses, folds and shelters – to honour the deer, and with the notable beauty of their inhabitants they were normally arranged as elegant eyecatchers.

Prince Pückler Muskau, who toured the country in 1827, describes the idiosyncrasies of the British and the chase:

The most striking thing to German eyes is the sight of the black-coated parsons, flying over hedge and ditch. I am told they often go to the church, ready booted and spurred, with the hunting whip in their hands, throw on a surplice, marry, christen or bury, with all conceivable velocity, jump on their horses at the church door, and off – tally-ho! They told me of a famous clerical fox-hunter, who always carried a tame fox in his pocket, that if they did not happen to find one they might be sure of a run. The animal was so well trained that he amused the hounds for a time; and when he was tired of running, took refuge in his inviolable retreat – which was no other than the altar of the Parish Church. There was a hole broken for him in the church wall, and a comfortable bed under the steps. This is right English religion.

Horses and hounds were handsomely housed. Sir James Miller of Manderston in Berwickshire settled his horses in generous opulence six years before he rebuilt his own house, spending £25,000 on his stables in 1895. The Milton Pack hunts from an eighteenth-century sham ruin to this day, and in Northumberland a Gothic castle was built for the dogs. Coursing, an offshoot of hunting, also produced many notable buildings. It generally took place in an enclosure about a mile long and half a mile wide, with the spectators assembled either at the 'Pinching Post' or in the 'Grandstand'. At Swarkeston in Derbyshire there is a pavilion, but the enclosure is small and it has been suggested that it was used also for bull-baiting. Both sports were relished by Elizabeth I, as well as bear-baiting, with which she was always 'well content'.

Fishing, by comparison, seems the most gentle and agreeable of pastimes. 'Never yet have I met an angler who was not a genial man', wrote James John Hissey in *Across England in a Dog Cart* (1891), 'and I wish all the fraternity a light heart and a heavy creel'. The love of the sport produced buildings of great stateliness and style: pavilions and temples seemingly afloat on the water's edge, the little square fishing tabernacles at Studley Royal in Yorkshire, the spiky, castellated 'Fort Henry' at Exton in Rutland, the Chinese fishing temple at Virginia Water – all have the most lively architectural spirit.

Under 'The Stomach' are dwellings built for creatures that eventually come to or provide for the dining table: beehouses, beehives and beeboles; houses for doves, duck and hens; cowsheds, pigsties and sheepfolds.

Doves have had houses of their own since Roman times, when men were employed specially to chew white bread to feed to the young birds, and even 'towns' were built to house them, and described by Pliny, Varro and Columella. These little buildings produced meat and eggs, as well as medicaments and manure, all the year round, and they flourished until well into the eighteenth century. Architectural gems, they are miniature representations of the vernacular for each county – crow-stepped in Caithness, gabled in Gloucestershire, timber-framed in Hereford, limestone in Oxford, red sandstone in Leicestershire, yellow in Shropshire. There are oddities, like the cones at Castletown and Rathfarnham in Ireland, the ornamental bright brick and stone 'pepperpot' at Cliveden in Buckinghamshire, and the urned and pedimented folly at Huntingdon House in East Lothian. They are round, square, octagonal, hexagonal, oblong and cruciform, with lanterns, castellations, spires, 'beehives', and towers. The beehive itself, even smaller, was often just as architecturally adventurous, with tiny Indian or Chinese temples, while the larger 'beehouses', with several hives, were built as ornamental summerhouses, and even as castles.

The fanciful results of the aesthetic and agricultural 'Age of Improvement' provided a perfect pretext for building evocative 'ruins' or 'Gothic temples' in which to house farm animals. Enthusiasm was rampant for experiment. In *Georgian Model Farms* (1983), John Martin Robinson gives us a description of a 'combined cow-shed and greenhouse' in which the plants were heated by the beasts' breath, the only ventilation for them being a hole in front of their noses leading into the glass-house.

The Duke of Portland built classical cowsheds with pierced ball finials; Adam designed a castle for cows in Ayr, as did William Kent in Oxfordshire; and the Duke of Norfolk built a most singular cowhouse in Cumberland – multi-towered, with stone 'petal' crowns, to impress his neighbour, a man of startling habits who kept his mistress's head in a glass box as a memento. Prince Albert, 'Prince among farmers as well as among peers', built model farms at Windsor, just half a mile away from one of the most sumptuously decorated rooms in Britain, the Royal Dairy, built for Queen Victoria by Prince Albert and John Thomas. Elihu Burritt, the American Consul in Birmingham, visited in 1865, and left a jewel of nineteenth-century flamboyant prose:

The Queen's Dairy! How Saxon and homelike that term! The Queen's cows 'with the crumpled horns'; brindled cows, spotted, red faced, white faced, mottled, brown and dun, coming in from the pasture at eve with whisking tails, and eyes soft, gentle, round and honest. The Queen's Milk-maids ... The Queen herself, in straw bonnet and thick-soled shoes, walking up and down the dairy-room, dropping heavy and smiling looks into pails and pans of milk and cream ... The walls, the long white marble tables, the fountains, the statuary of rustic life, and all the finely-sculptured allegories look as if wrought from new milk petrified just as the cream began to rise to the surface or as if, looking into the basined pools of the soft white fluid circling around the interior, like great fluent pearls strung for a bracelet, they had gradually assimilated themselves to the medium that reflected their faces, and had taken up both its softness of look and sweetness of savor.

Under the heading 'Decoration' I have examined animal houses that are primarily ornamental, such as bird-cages or aviaries, but it has also been most useful as an umbrella heading for all that defy categorisation. How can a temple for terrapins be classified? Or a black castle for bears in the middle of Leeds? Decoration will do, although it applies to the whole book, with gleaming knobs on.

The aviary at Kenilworth was brilliant with 'jewels'. In 1575 it was described by John Laneham as 'sumptuous and beautiful', 'of a rare form and excellence'. Twenty feet high, thirty long, and fourteen deep, with eight great 'wyndoz', it was 'beautifyed with great Diamons, Emeraulds, Rubyes, and Saphyres ... garnisht with their golld by skilfull hed and hand'. These giant cages flourished for another four hundred years, with such architects as Thomas Wright and John Plaw allowing the inmates to give their designers exotic licence to build the most fantastical temples in honour of the birds.

The same taste for the exotic was behind the building of a Chinoiserie monkey-house at Culzean and a zebra harnessing-room at Tring, which shafted up three zebras and a pony to pull the Rothschilds' trap to London. The first menagerie in Britain had been at Woodstock, where Henry I had lions, lynxes, leopards, camels and a porcupine. Henry III later moved them all to the Tower of London, where animals were to be kept for the next five hundred years in dank and fetid conditions, virtually underground in a circular pit of stone arches. There was a white bear, thought to be albino rather than Polar, who was allowed out daily, on a long rope, to fish in the Thames. The first elephant to come to the country lived in the Tower from 1254, and the first rhinoceros was sent there in 1739. A grim detail is that the public could bring a live dog or cat to be fed to the animals in lieu of payment.

Exeter 'Change was the next great menagerie to be opened to the public. From 1773 to 1829 its respective owners, Pidcock, Polito and Cross, kept their wretched animals, including an elephant and a lion, in tiny cages above the shops in the Strand. The only concession to their former life in the wild were murals of tropical foliage painted around the walls.

When London Zoo was opened, it boasted 'the most extensive assemblage of living Quadrupeds and Birds ever exhibited in this, or perhaps any other, country'. The Zoological Society had been founded in 1825 by Sir Stamford Raffles with the support of Sir Humphry Davy, and plans were immediately drawn up to create a place where 'individuals of more expanded views' could enlarge their knowledge of nature 'through closer examination of her works'. The Tower and Cross menageries looked after the animals, housed in the Elysium at Regent's Park, and on 27 April 1828 the five acres of gardens were opened to the public. There were elephants, monkeys in a domed monkey-house, llamas in what is now the camel-house, by Decimus Burton, who also built the macaw-cage and the giraffe-house. The zoo has grown to thirty-six acres, and has continued to keep robustly apace with architectural improvements. Lubetkin and Tecton built the gorilla-house in 1933, and their penguin pool of a year later was startlingly innovatory with its interlacing, self-supporting concrete ramps. The elephants were housed by Sir Hugh Casson in 1965, and the birds in the soaring aviary by Lord Snowdon in the same year. The nineteenth-century aviary still survives.

'Death' is the sumptuous finale, boasting a glittering array of memorials and monuments to tortoises, monkeys, wombats, pigs, carrier-pigeons, rabbits, robins, dogs, horses ... and a tomb to a trout.

Keith Thomas tells us, in *Man and the Natural World* (1983), of Samuel Clarke in the late seventeenth century, who thought it probable 'that the souls of brutes would eventually be resurrected and lodged in Mars, Saturn or some other Planet', and of the Reverend Augustus Toplady, author of the hymn 'Rock of Ages', who declared in the 1770s, 'I firmly believe that beasts have souls; souls truly and properly so called.' An unnamed 'Divine' thought otherwise. He would allow vermin to bite him without hindrance: 'We shall have Heaven to reward us for all our sufferings, but these poor creatures have nothing but the enjoyment of this present life.' The Reverend J. G. Wood, on the other hand, who claimed to have tamed two butterflies through two winters, wrote hefty volumes on animal immortality: *Man and Beast Here and Hereafter* (1874). He had many letters of abuse. One – twelve pages of close-written, full-sized letter paper – told him that 'anyone who cherished the hope that animals could live after death was unworthy of his position as a clergyman, ought to be deprived of his university degrees, and expelled from the learned societies to which he belonged. This argument was so unanswerable that I did not venture to reply to it.' He was less reticent with another who wrote that 'he would never condescend to share immortality with a cheese-mite. I replied that, in the first place, it was not likely that he would be consulted on the subject; and that, in the second place, as he did condescend to share mortality with a good many cheese-mites, there could be no great harm in extending his condescension a step further.'

Perhaps he should have referred his indignant correspondents to a higher authority:

For that which befalleth the sons of man befalleth beasts; even one thing befalleth them: as the one dieth, so dieth the other; yea, they have all one breath; so that a man hath no pre-eminence above a beast: for all is vanity.

ECCLESIASTES 3:19

Chatelherault

The 'Dog Kennel' was designed by William Adam, father of Robert, for the Duke of Hamilton in about 1732. The combined kennels, hunting lodge, summer-house and garden pavilion stood as an eyecatcher to Hamilton Palace, the 'Chatsworth of the North' built by James Smith in 1684 and demolished in 1927. From the great gallery of the house, it closed the view through a mile-long double avenue of trees. Now it stands alone in the wrecked landscape of Hamilton, with only a gateway or two and the mausoleum in the valley below to remind us of the ducal splendours it once dominated. In 1548, James Hamilton, then Regent Arran, arranged the marriage between Mary Queen of Scots and the young Dauphin, and Henri II of France created him the Duc de Chatelherault.

The pavilion on the right was for the Duke and Duchess, with a banqueting room and their two apartments, encrusted with Rococo plasterwork.

Diana, the goddess of the hunt, is sitting in deep relief with her greyhound, surrounded by instruments of music and the chase. In the pavilion on the left lived the gardener and kennelman, with the hounds behind them. The façade is 280 feet long, and once fronted the hunting grounds known as the High Parks. Terraced gardens rose up behind the building which, sadly neglected for years, is now being restored. The Historic Buildings and Monuments Directorate of the Scottish Development Department are in charge, and the architects are Boys Jarvis Partnership. The sandstone is being dug from the original quarry, only yards from the kennels.

The buildings are covered with scaffolding and cannot be seen, but this illustration from *Vetruvius Scoticus* (1812) is in no way an idealisation. The colour of the stone and the grand scale make it even more extraordinary.

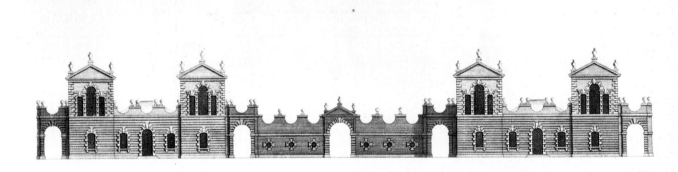

Generall Front toward the North of the Dogg Kennell att Hamilton. Situate att the head of the South Avenue a mile Distant from, & Fronting the Palace

Wil: Adam inv et delin

R: Cooper Sculp

Nunwick

The hound kennels at Nunwick in Northumberland were built in 1768 by Sir Lancelot Allgood MP, who was knighted when High Sheriff of Northumberland by George III. The little castle, prettily situated by the river, is to be seen as a romantic ruin from the house, a Georgian pile of 1750.

It is from here that a guinea fowl exercised daily with the hounds, racing along for ten miles or more. He went out hunting, too, and when exhausted would perch on the back of the huntsman's saddle as the chase jolted on. He is stuffed at Nunwick, with one claw missing, trodden off by a horse. And it was James Allgood, the 'Celebrated Gentleman Jock', riding under the assumed name of Captain Barlow (he was aspiring to the cloth, and it was thought unsuitable to have racing connections), who in the White Hart at Aylesbury, in 1830, committed the great feat of leaping his grey horse over a table laden with champagne: 'the horse jumped, the champagne glasses rattled, the plates quivered, the candlesticks shook, but nothing was displaced.'

13

Sherborne

Lodge Park, Sherborne, in Gloucestershire, a beautiful little building with its five broken pediments crammed onto the façade, is a grey-hound-coursing 'grandstand'. It was built *c.* 1650 for a John Dutton and is attributed to John Webb, whose contemporary drawing of the building survives in the RIBA. In the late seventeenth century it was thought to have been built by Inigo Jones.

Dutton, known as 'Crump' because of his hunchback, was gaoled twice for refusing to pay ship-money. He was a friend of Oliver Cromwell, who relished the sport of deer-coursing, and in 1655 obtained permission from the Lord Protector to stock his park at Sherborne with deer from Wychwood Forest. He was described as a 'learned and prudent man ... one of the richest ... meekest men in England' (*Athenae Oxonienses*), which tallies oddly with the tale of his staking Sherborne at the gaming table, whence he had to be forcibly dragged by his butler, who had been startled into action by the cry 'Sherborne is up'.

Originally there were only two rooms to the lodge, running the full length of the building: the hall downstairs, and the room leading onto the balcony above. There were two fireplaces up-stairs, each with a great stone overmantel in the shape of a shell. The grandstand, enclosure and beech spinney (still surviving, a mile away), from which the deer were 'slipped', could be used by anyone who would pay for the day's sport – half a crown for the dog, twelve pence to the 'slipper'. Lodge Park was converted into a dwelling-house in 1898, by Emma, Lady Sherborne.

Loudon's Kennels

The kennels for pointers and hounds in the 'Italian' (*above*) and the 'Tudor Gothic' (*below*) manner were designed by Mr Lamb in the early nineteenth century for John Claudius Loudon's *Encyclopaedia of Cottage, Farm and Villa Architecture* (1833), where it is suggested the curving walls be replaced by railings, 'it being found ... that dogs are always quietest when their kennels command an extensive prospect'.

Inside were a show room, breeding rooms, a boiling house, 'hospitals', areas for carcases and for coal, a reservoir supplied by a spring, and yards, all sloping with irrigating channels cut into the stone.

Loudon writes that architects designing country buildings should 'take hints for the general forms and dispositions of the masses, from the ground on which they are and from the surrounding scenery', even to the humblest building, so that it would seem as if they had grown out of the ground, 'instead of appearing to have been brought there from some town or village'.

Canine Residences

The Residences for a Canine Family in Modern Times (*above*) and Ancient Times (*below*) are designs commissioned by the Earl Bishop of Derry from John Soane in 1788, when the architect was only twenty-five years old. Soane was in Italy gathering both knowledge and patrons, and after visiting the Villa Lucullus with the Earl Bishop, where there were no kennels to be found, he was asked to produce what might have been and what splendours could yet be built – perhaps under Irish skies.

They are temples to the glory of the hunt, of a grandeur that was thought ridiculous by many, including William Somerville:

> First let the kennel be the huntsman's care
> Upon some little eminence erect,
> And fronting to the ruddy dawn ...
> Let no Corinthian pillars prop the dome,
> A vain expense, on charitable deeds
> Better dispos'd ... For use, not state
> Gracefully plain, let each apartment rise ...

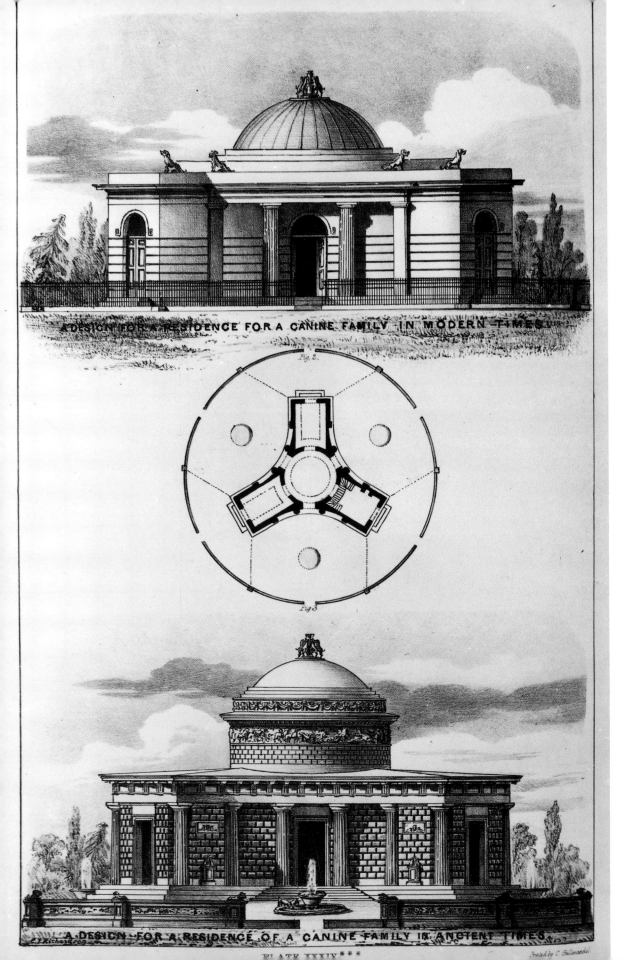

A DESIGN FOR A RESIDENCE FOR A CANINE FAMILY IN MODERN TIMES.

A DESIGN FOR A RESIDENCE OF A CANINE FAMILY IN ANCIENT TIMES.

West Wycombe

The cockpit at West Wycombe Park in Buckinghamshire was built by Sir Francis Dashwood of the notorious Hell-Fire Club, no doubt to encourage more of the lustful delight in pleasure and depravity enjoyed by his fellow members. The motto of the 'Knights of St Francis of Wycombe', as they were called, 'LIBERTATI AMICITIAE Q SAC SACRUM', is inscribed over the arch. They were an illustrious bunch. John Wilkes, Sir William Stanhope and Lord Sandwich, First Lord of the Admiralty, were among the politicians, pamphleteers and poets who revelled in licentious and satanic rites in the caves that Sir Francis had excavated deep in the hills of West Wycombe and in the semi-ruined abbey of Medmenham. Each had a cell to retire to, in monk's habit, for 'private devotions', and beneath the obscenely frescoed ceilings of the chapel Black Masses would frequently be held. Masked women dressed as nuns were part of the extraordinary scenes, commanded to be lively and cheerful, to add to the 'general hilarity' of the occasions!

The cockpit was all part of the fun – and part, too, of the more distinguished side of Sir Francis's character. He was a founder member of the Dilettanti Society, formed to promote the arts, and was himself an exuberant builder. 'If not superfluous, at least profuse' was a polite description of the landscape he created between 1750 and 1780, dotted hither and thither with monuments, temples, pavilions and bridges. He employed Nicholas Revett, John Donovell and Robert Adam, who built the stables, to which the flint niche beyond, with its statue of Apollo Belvedere, acts as a screen.

The Tuscan-arched cockpit stands only yards from the house. Built of flint with stucco dressings, it houses its vile sport in a room above the arch. An engraving by Hogarth of the same date shows the full horror of the greed for cruelty encouraged by cock-fighting, with men falling over each other to leer at the wretched combatants. Boswell went to a cockfight in London in 1762, where the birds 'armed with silver heels' fought 'with amazing bitterness and resolution ... one pair fought for three-quarters of an hour ... I was sorry for the poor cocks. I looked round to see if any of the spectators pitied them when mangled and torn in a most cruel manner, but I could not observe the smallest relenting sign in any countenance.' In 1835 an Act of Parliament was passed making cock-fighting illegal.

Brockelesby

The Wyatt kennels for the Earl of Yarborough's hounds at Brockelesby in Lincolnshire were built in the 1780s. The pack is a private one, and the building is still immaculate and in brisk working order. The stone of the walls and floors, the dark blue of the wood and ironwork and the mass of hounds make the most pleasing picture. Wonderful old-fashioned names are still in use: Wellington, Captain, Careful, Stately, Colonel, Comely and Charmer.

The huntsmen live in the central house, and four towers surround the yards. Two are 'hospital lodges', and the others are for the puppies and the kennel staff. A small fireplace and bath were provided for the driver of the 'knackers car'. The stone flags on all the floors are enormous and spanking clean. In one room, with two giant boilers, oatcakes are mixed and laid out on the stone to cool; in another, with a slate floor, the cakes are put out of the way to set.

A grim chamber has an ancient board devoted to some hundreds of dead foxes – the snouts and whiskers of every one caught since 1882 are there, with the dates of the killing.

This is the oldest private pack in the country, dating from 1714. Always an active hunting family, the Pelhams saw to it that each evening after dinner the butler would announce, 'The horses are bedded, my Lord.' The gentlemen would then progress to the stables along a covered passage in which a fireplace had been built especially for this little journey.

Bavington

The dovecote, greyhound-coursing pavilion and mock-ruin eyecatcher standing in the open country at Bavington in Northumberland has been used, within living memory, for coursing dogs and keeping birds.

Greyhound-coursing, chasing the deer, the hare and the fox, has been popular since ancient times, when wolves and boars would also have been the quarry. It remained a privileged and private pursuit until 1776, when Lord Orford instituted the first public meetings of the Swaffham Coursing Club in Norfolk. Following this example, the entertainments, with their new and official rules and regulations, flourished all over the country, open to all and sundry, in the nineteenth century developing into an increasingly popular pastime, both town and country dwellers taking an active interest. A familiar sight to this day is a Northumberland or Durham miner exercising his elegant hounds.

The first course to be laid down for the hunting of the artificial hare was at Hendon, in a field behind the Welsh Harp, in October 1876.

Milton

Hounds have been kennelled at Milton, near Peterborough, since the reign of Richard II, when the Abbot of Peterborough was given the right to hunt in the surrounding Royal forests. The hounds are thought originally to have come from Bordeaux, under the auspices of Sir Bernard Brocas, friend of the King. After the Dissolution of the Monasteries they were put into the hands of the Fitzwilliams, where they have remained ever since. The family have lived at Milton since 1500 and the hunt has been one of the 'Governing Packs' of England (the Belvoir and the Brockelesby are others), which means that most other packs in the country have been bred from them. Sadly for the hound historian, the kennels were destroyed by fire in 1760, and with them all the pedigree books.

Sir William Chambers and Humphrey Repton have both been attributed with the design of this sham 'ruin'. Chambers was commissioned to build an orangery and a temple in 1771; Repton made proposals for relandscaping at the same time; and it is thought that both he and John Nash designed the enchanting Gothic lodge that stands in the park.

The kennels are in brisk use today, with thirty-eight and a half 'entered' couples (hounds that have been hunted), and fourteen and a half couples of puppies. There are three yards behind these castellations, and three 'lodges' (where the hounds sleep), two 'draw yards' (where they are sorted out) and one 'feed house', where 'fallen stock' given to the hunt by local farmers is fed to the pack daily.

The valeting room in the tower, where boots, coats and whips are cleaned, is painted from floor to ceiling with Masters, horses and the 'old favourites' of the hounds. Earl Fitzwilliam and Major Warre are portrayed at a puppy show, and Mr Rex Sly, Mrs Bridget Raby and Sir Stephen and Lady Hastings are at an opening meet. Countess Fitzwilliam is also a joint Master. George Adams, in the photograph, is the huntsman today.

Sudbury

The deer-house at Sudbury Hall in Derbyshire was built in 1723, and at that time it was plastered and painted white. The corner towers had ogee domes, there was no gaunt 'Tudor gatehouse' and in 1750 it was thatched. This quaint and picturesque eighteenth-century deercote *ornée* was transformed into a toy fort, probably by the early 1800s. It stands in what was once the deer park created by Mistress Mary Vernon, in 1614. She had begun to build the first house at Sudbury a year earlier and had laid out the great deer park, some three miles round, as part of the estate. Her steward, Hardstaffe, made a poetic record of the operation:

> The old Blackmore (enlarged with some more
>   ground)
> Was with a strong high pale encompaste
>   round.
> The purpose was (as shortly did appeare)
> To make a Parke for redd and fallowe deere.

The goings on in the seventeenth century would have been grim and bloody, with a terrible elegance. R. Blowe, in the *Gentleman's Recreation* of 1686, writes of 'The death of the stag with the ceremonies to be observed therein … He that gives the falling blow, ought of righte to sound the Recheat to assemble together the rest of the company … the Huntsman presents the person that took the Essay, with a drawn Hanger to have a Chop of his Head, and after him everyone hath a chop if it is not cut off; and generally the Huntsman or keeper is provided with such a Hanger that is not over/Sharp, that there may be more chops for the gaining more fees, everyone giving him a shilling at least.' James I would slit the deer's throat himself and smear the blood on his courtiers, and the greatest privilege a lady could hope for in the field was to make the first cut herself and to wash her hands in the blood.

Coatham Mundeville

In the late eighteenth or early nineteenth century a tiny crowstepped castle for deer was designed as a pleasing eyecatcher across the fields from Hallgarth, at Coatham Mundeville in County Durham.

By this time, the fox had become the huntsman's prey, and deer were the most admired ornaments to every parkland. As early as 1774, Oliver Goldsmith was censuring 'the chase', which 'continued in many parts of the country where the red deer is still preserved and still makes the amusement of such as have not found out more liberal entertainments.' Practices of the vilest cruelty had become acceptable, with the 'carted stag' having its leg dislocated or broken, or even one foot cut off, being borne off to the spot of 'release' where the dogs would be ready and waiting. 'Where is the unnatural, base, grovelling, grinning, pimping scoundrel who can put his unfeeling claws to the act of grinding dislocation?' wrote 'Humanitas' of the *Sporting Magazine* in the early 1800s.

Belvoir

The hound kennels at Belvoir Castle, built in 1802, were more than likely one of the collaborated designs of the Fifth Duchess of Rutland and James Wyatt, who worked on the remodelling of the castle between 1801 and 1813. (It was rebuilt by Thoroton after a fire in 1816, with interiors by Wyatt's two sons.)

At the time of the kennels being built, the Belvoir Hunt was emerging from a quiet phase. The Fifth Duke had inherited when he was only nine, and over the next twelve years the famous pack had ground to a virtual halt. Then, in the 1790s, the Trustees had been galvanised into action, and a new master was appointed. Hounds were bred with, among others, the Milton pack (q.v.), and new couples were added. In 1805, the Duke became Master and took on a celebrated huntsman, 'Gentleman Shaw', of 'superior attainments and possibly of superior birth', who was in his glory, his face 'alight with pleasure', when 'the chiming pack, heads up and sterns down, started to race over the grass.'

The kennels are now in active use, with sixty couples. There are four 'lodges', four yards, and the 'Duke's Room', where the hounds were inspected by the Duke of Rutland. He suffered from gout, and sat like a museum exhibit behind railings (to protect him from the hounds) in an armchair by the fire, the animals being let in and out through a draught-free trapdoor.

Teasel, the labrador of today's huntsman, Mr Robin Jackson, is posing in the photograph.

Dunham Massey

The deer-house at Dunham Massey in Cheshire, built by George Booth, Second Earl of Warrington, is oddly undecorative, considering that he classicised the Tudor house and planted in the park a hundred thousand trees of oak, elm and beech. The Earl also built an obelisk to his mother and an orangery in the garden.

Deer-hunting was on the decline by the mid-eighteenth century. With the increased cultivation of land, wild herds were disappearing and deer parks alone remained, often with half-tame creatures to be pursued.

The park at Dunham Massey has medieval origins and was enclosed for deer-hunting well before the reign of Elizabeth I. It has retained an ancient atmosphere – no 'Picturesque' hands were ever let loose on the Earl of Warrington's planting. When criticised for his extravagance, he replied,

'Gentlemen, you may think it strange that I do these things; but I have the inward satisfaction in my own breast; the benefit of posterity and my survivors will receive more than double the profit, than by any other method I would possibly take for their interest.'

There are 240 deer in the park today. According to Ormerod's 1882 survey of Cheshire the land had supported as many as 500. By the 1750s the chase rather than the kill had become the glory: 'carted' animals were set free ('breathed'), given ten minutes 'law', then pursued by the 'stop-dogs'. When it was caught, the stag would be saved from death by the 'yeoman-prickers', hunt servants in brilliant livery of scarlet jackets laced with gold who would plunge into the fray and ward off the hounds. Often a 'Teazer' would start the deer off, a mongrel greyhound that was 'slipt' first.

Loudon's Stables

'The domestic quadrupeds … are chiefly the horse, the cow, the sheep, and the swine … taken in the plan, or vertical profile, they are all more or less wedge-shaped; the head being placed at the narrow end of the wedge.' These stables in the 'Italian' (*above*) and the 'Tudor Gothic' (*below*) styles exemplify the tapering 'wedge' described by John Claudius Loudon in his *Encyclopaedia of Cottage, Farm and Villa Architecture* (1833). Each had a central yard for 'young horses to run loose in occasionally'. There were six stables for saddle horses, four for coach horses, six for hunters, and two others, one with two stalls, the other a single. On the first floor, with the lofts for hay and corn, was a billiard room.

The flat roofs were recommended both because they were much cheaper and because they gave the building a more imposing character. The encircling colonnade, nearly 200 feet in circumference, was for exercising horses and for riding and driving in bad weather.

The stables were built for a Colonel Mytton of Garth, Montgomeryshire, in the early 1800s, but the 'elevation actually executed from our Design was different from either', wrote Loudon, 'and, we need not say, much inferior'.

Charing Cross

The Royal Stables at Charing Cross were built by William Kent between 1731 and 1733. They took up the western half of where the National Gallery stands today, and overlooked the 'Great Mews', now Trafalgar Square. This 'Prospective View' is a little squashed as there was, in fact, a block of over twenty houses, including a riding house, Mr Montague's stable and an 'extensive' granary between the church of St Martin-in-the-Fields and the stable block.

It is thought that Edward I was the earliest king to keep his horses in the 'Muwes', and it is recorded that Thomas de Erleham, the royal Keeper, was paid nine pence a day. The King's falcons and falconers were also housed here.

The stables were rebuilt between 1547 and 1559. Sir Christopher Wren was asked to make new designs at the end of the seventeenth century, and so too was Nicholas Hawksmoor, but they were not rebuilt again until 1731. They had been in constant use over the years. Wren noted that horses were housed there in 1686, and his plans were for eighty-eight more, as well as forty-two coaches.

There was always a large 'horse pond' in the middle of what is now Trafalgar Square. In the late eighteenth century there were also an enormous barn for hay and straw, a blacksmith, an engine-house, stables and coach-houses on its eastern side. To the south were two coach-houses, an alehouse and a 'men's gate house', and almost the entire western block was made up of more stables.

Behind Kent's monumental 'rustick' façade, around a court called the Green Mews, stood a wood-yard, yet more stables, coach-houses and a garden. The proposals of 1731 were eventually to cost some £14,000, George II's wish to be able to walk between his horses doubling both the size of the building and the initial estimate of £6,000. The arched stables, with their soaring piers and pilasters, eventually faced one another, where originally there was to have been a single row. They were demolished in 1830, having in their declining years been used as a menagerie.

The word 'mews' comes from the old French word *muer*, which in turn came from the Latin *mutare*, 'to change'. Mews were for falcons in the Middle Ages, and were so called because of the 'mewing', or moulting, of the birds' plumage.

29

Bishop Auckland

The deer-house in the demesne of the Bishop's Palace at Bishop Auckland dates from 1760. It was built by Bishop Trevor (Bishop of Durham from 1759 to 1771), a saintly man of 'singular dignity ... tall, well proportioned, and of a carriage erect and stately. The Episcopal robe was never worn more gracefully.' He employed Sir Thomas Robinson to design a gateway to Auckland Castle. It is presumed that the deer-house, with its similar Gothic spikes and castellations, is by the same hand. The arches, marching along to the corner buttresses, allowed the deer into the enclosed courtyard, where they could shelter and be fed during the winter. The central tower had an upper room in which one could sit and watch the deer below. It cost £379 to build.

Bishop Trevor met with a grim death. On 10 March 1771 he was attacked by gangrene, 'and a mortification of the most fatal kind ensued; the toes sloughed off one after another ... the bark was taken ... in as large quantities as ever known ... but it was too malignant and had already taken a mortal hold.'

Peover

Astonishingly, everything to do with the stables at Peover Hall in Cheshire – the Tuscan columns, the strapwork and the plaster – is original. Peover, the seat of the Mainwaring family from the Norman Conquest until the twentieth century, went through a particularly grand stage in the 1660s, when Sir Philip Mainwaring was secretary to the doomed Duke of Stafford. Van Dyke painted a portrait of them together. Ellen Mainwaring, who had married his son, built the stables in 1654, with the inscription above the door proclaiming them, 'The gift of Mrs Ellen Mainwaring to her son Thomas Mainwaring Esq.'

It is thought that the craftsmen who worked here were the same as those who carved the chapel screen at Cholmondeley Castle nearby, in 1655. They are oddly alike, with strapwork arches marching along at the foot of the altar, but Cholmondeley has Corinthian rather than Doric capitals.

Before the mid-century cruelty to horses had been commonplace, with such alarming practices as tying a live hedgehog under the horse's tail or 'blazing straw about their ears'. They were ridden into the ground and discarded in their thousands. In the seventeenth century their lot changed. The horse cost more than a human servant to keep and often was more sumptuously housed. When Colonel Holmes, a supporter of Monmouth, was to be executed in 1685, the cart for the condemned men proved too heavy for the horses. 'Come gentlemen', said Holmes, 'don't let the poor creatures suffer on our account. I have often led you in the field. Let me lead you on our way to Heaven.'

Seaton Delaval

When the 1768 stables of Seaton Delaval, the great Palladian palace which stands in the bleak industrial landscape of south Northumberland, were finished, Sir Francis Delaval held a banquet in them to celebrate their beauty. The house and the West Wing were built between 1718 and 1732 by Sir John Vanbrugh for Admiral George Delaval, but neither man lived to see them finished and it was left to Sir Francis, the Admiral's dashing great-nephew, to complete the desired symmetry by building the East Wing, the stable block, twenty-six years later, basing his plans on those for the stables at Hopetoun near Edinburgh.

Sir Francis, one of thirteen children known as the 'Gay Delavals' for their colourful and distinguished pursuits, was the most dazzling of all: an MP, Knight of the Bath, soldier and elegant dilettante, he also found time to stage magnificent theatricals. He played the title role in his production of *Othello*, and was given the Drury Lane Theatre for the evening by Garrick, Parliament being adjourned two hours early for the performance. He loved practical jokes, and devilish devices to lower beds into tanks of icy cold water were installed at Seaton Delaval, as well as walls that slid away revealing the next-door bedroom. The stables were his last great act of extravagance at a time when the now sombre house was like an Italian palace and the grounds were a 'perfect fairyland of light, beauty and music'. They are a triumph.

The 'grand stable' measures sixty-eight by thirty-five feet, with three magnificent arches rising to the full height of the building, the central one spanning an apse with a Venetian window looking out onto the stable yard. There are twelve stalls for the horses, with lead-lined feeding troughs and arched niches above for the hay hecks. The names of the first twelve horses to live here, in the 1760s, are elegantly written above the keystone of each niche: Zephyrus, Hercules, Tartar, Regulus, Peacock, Julius, Chance, Prince, Pilot, Fox, Captain and Steady.

Penicuik

The stables of Penicuik House, Mid Lothian, built by Sir James Clerk in the 1760s, can be seen through the portico of the great Palladian house, which was gutted by fire on 16 June 1899.

Sir James inherited the estate in 1755 with Newbiggin House. His father, Sir John Clerk, had been too fond of the old hall to make alterations – 'Better in its antique figure than if it was all new built' – and had concentrated on improving the estate. In the naturally beautiful setting beneath the Pentland Hills, with the valley of the North Esk cutting deeply through, he planted over 300,000 trees between 1700 and 1730. He created lakes and built follies, a bridge, a tunnel with an underground room and a pavilion. The way was clear for his son to set a palace down in this perfect landscape.

With James Baxter, a master builder who would transpose his ideas into technically viable plans, Sir James began work on the house and the stables in 1761. A building of spirit and distinction in its own right, the stable was unusual in that it was built bang in front of the house. The arched portico beneath the clock steeple leads through into an open courtyard facing the pedimented arch supporting Arthurs O'on (q.v.). The stable block formed one side, the coach-house, the brewhouse and the bakehouse the others. Circular stairs were built in all four corners, making the walls bulge out where the angles should be.

In 1899, after the fire, the architects Lessels and Taylor were employed to make the stables habitable, since the full insurance could not be paid on the house, which was still standing. Statuary, door-cases and fireplaces (one from Newbiggin House) were moved from the ruin. The statues had been commissioned from Italy by Sir James Clerk in the 1760s. Today, with a fountain echoing in the courtyard, now planted as a bright garden and watched over by the tall spire and the hump of Arthurs O'on, the atmosphere is rare and strange.

Buckingham Palace

The Royal Mews at Buckingham Palace were built by John Nash between 1822 and 1825. George III had bought Buckingham House in 1762 but had continued to use the magnificent stables at Charing Cross (q.v.) as his main quarters. Those at Buckingham House became known as the Queen's Mews and sixty years later, when George IV was forced by the proposals of the New Street Commission to rehouse his horses, the Queen's Stables were the natural choice for rebuilding. Nash submitted an estimate for £49,124 18s 6d in June 1822, and work began in July. There were many complications and delays, and when three years later Nash could pronounce them finished, 'constructed in a substantial and durable manner', they had cost almost £20,000 more than the original estimate.

Today, with thirty animals and as many men, this village devoted to horses is an extraordinary enclave in the middle of London, mysteriously cut off from all sound of the surrounding traffic, with an atmosphere of smooth-running hard work performed with tremendous pride. There are coach-houses full of State Coaches and Landaus, Broughams, Sociables, Barouches, Phaetons and Victorias, all kept in perfect repair, and the finest collection of 'horse furniture', with the eight sets of State harness for George III's golden coach, richly encrusted with gilt ormolu, and others such as the 'Black Horse Harness', decorated with brass.

All the stable ranges around Nash's courtyard are of mellow green, blue and white. The main stables, with their thirty-two stalls beneath sixteen arches, have drinking troughs with a ballcock and automatic flushing drains. The herringbone central aisle was once sanded, and until 1982 was edged with a 'Norfolk Plait', a straw mat three feet deep which was rolled up at night and put down in the morning to provide a clean edge between the sand and the straw. It has been replaced with a 'doormat' just one foot deep. The names of the horses, all chosen by the Queen, are still painted on the plaques above the stalls today, many with their foaling year. All are Windsor Greys or Cleveland Bays.

Welbeck Abbey

The Riding School (*above*) and Tan Gallop (*below*) at Welbeck Abbey in Nottingham are both part of the vast building programme from 1857 to 1878 of the eccentric Fifth Duke of Portland, who lived a good deal of the time underground, coming up enthusiastically to supervise the construction of the magnificent 'village' he was building for himself, his tenants and his animals. He built a series of underground rooms attached to the house, all painted pink, and all enormous, including a ballroom 154 by 64 feet. There were two underground tunnels leading to the Riding School, one for the Duke, the other for the workmen. Another, wide enough for two carriages to pass, was excavated for nearly a mile to the edge of the estate.

The Duke built a prodigious number of buildings for his animals, all equally splendid. There were hunting stables covering an acre, coach stables, racehorse stables and fire stables. At the ring of the alarm bell the fireman would slide down the brass pole and with a flick of his hand release complete harnesses suspended from the ceiling. Down they would drop, onto the horses' backs, just one buckle to do up on each before they were off, with six horses pulling a brass boiler.

The glass-roofed Tan Gallop was 422 yards long ('tan', the outer shell of a coconut, split and shredded into strands, was laid thick on the ground), while the Riding School was thought to be second in size only to that in Moscow, which was 'capable of holding two cavalry regiments, both manoeuvring at the same time.' It measures 385 by 112 feet and is fifty-two feet high. The outside is neo-Tudor, built of limestone quarried on the estate, with eight urned gables and strapwork on the walls and doors. Its heaviness is totally at odds with the delicacy of the interior, although the immaculate greensward of the Welbeck land does lend it dignity. The Sixth Duke and the Duchess rode here until the Second World War, always in top hat and full side-saddle habit.

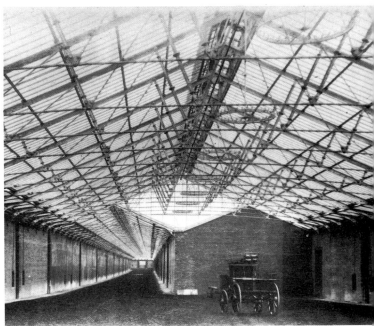

Berkeley

The Gothic brick stables at Berkeley Castle in Gloucestershire, home of the Berkeley Hunt, were built in the late eighteenth and early nineteenth century. With the kennels that stand across the yard, they are the headquarters of the oldest hunt in England. It was founded in 1067, when Roger de Berkeley was given lands by William the Conqueror after the Battle of Hastings, and for the next seven and a half centuries hunted within a radius that grew to span the lands between the banks of the River Severn and the heights of Islington and Highgate, some 130 miles apart.

There is a fourteenth-century account of a Lord Berkeley following the buck through Charing village (now Charing Cross), and another of Henry, Lord Berkeley, hunting at Gray's Inn in 1555. At the end of the eighteenth century, a fox found by a Berkeley huntsman in Wormwood Scrubs was later lost in Kensington Gardens. All the hunt servants would have been dressed, as they are today, in yellow coats, with silver foxes with golden brushes embroidered on their black lapels.

Throughout this far-flung territory, which included parts of Gloucestershire, Warwickshire, Oxfordshire, Northamptonshire, Leicestershire, Buckinghamshire, Berkshire and Middlesex, there were kennels at Gerrards Cross, and even, it is thought, at Charing Cross. At Cranford in Middlesex, the old hunt building, with its little Dutch gable, still survives, only feet from the westbound M4 and hard by Heathrow Airport. There were kennels, too, at Nettlebed and at Cheltenham.

In the early 1800s, these lands were split in two, one becoming the 'London territory'. The pack, known as the Old Berkeley until 1970, has now amalgamated with other packs, and hunts as the Vale of Aylesbury, with a similar yellow coat.

The Berkeley Hunt, based in Gloucestershire, continued to pursue the chase in its depleted territory, which still covered some 350 square miles. One keen follower, a yeoman farmer named Jack Hawkins, lived on the Welsh side of the River Severn and in his eagerness to hunt with the pack would swim over the water hanging on to his horse's tail. These journeys were so regular that contemporary ordnance survey maps would have 'Jack Hawkins Esq.' spanning the Severn like a bridge.

The Berkeley stables are delicate and pretty, with ten Gothic doorways and ten Gothic windows. Above the central arched doorway which divides them is a window inset with a black and gold clock. The roof is castellated.

The back of this building is an eyecatcher to be seen across the meadows from Berkeley Castle. Faced with stone, it has two storeys of diamond-latticed Gothic windows and taller castellations.

Hovingham Hall

From the front door of Hovingham Hall in Yorkshire can be seen one of the most curious architectural views in England. Although in the house, you are in fact standing in the stables and looking out into the riding school. It is all part of Thomas Worsley's grand equine plan built between 1752 and 1769 so that his horses could be housed on the ground floor of his own home. Hovingham Hall stands in the middle of the village of Hovingham, with a rusticated entrance arch overlooking the green. Suspecting nothing,

one walks into the tunnel-vaulted passage to be confronted by an immense arched and columned riding school, sweeping you up to the front door, which in turn leads you into the groin-vaulted stables. There are three stone apartments: the Samson Hall, with its baseless Tuscan columns and floor of hexagonal oak blocks suitable for carriages; and two vaulted ranges, one on either side, both with stone floors and columns with hefty bases and restrained capitals. The Samson Hall was called after Giambologna's marble 'Samson and the Philistine' which once stood between the columns.

Arthur Young, the agricultural critic and diarist, visited Hovingham in 1709 and wrote of the new architectural arrangements with alarm: 'Nothing should be condemned because uncommon, but I should apprehend with some horses, that it might hazard the necks of many a coachful, if the ladies persisted in not walking this approach.' He was equally critical of the layout of the *piano nobile* with its magnificent Doric Room and the Ballroom leading onto a balcony, from where the company could watch the horses being trained in the riding school below. 'I should remark that this room opens onto a small gallery, which has windows into the riding house, and as that communicates immediately with four or five stables, I should suppose that when they are well stocked with horses in hot weather, it would be easy enough to *smell* without being *told* these two rooms (the best in the house) are built over the apartments of the "Houghnhnms".' Thomas Worsley enjoyed his horses 'daily and without fear'. He was judged to be one of the best riders of his day, and in 1769 he wrote, 'horses … are my music and thank God I have yet a hand and an ear for them.'

He turned this hand happily to architecture, and has been credited with the design of the riding house of the Royal Mews at Buckingham Palace – as well as the plan of those bold and curious arrangements at Hovingham.

Hope End

All that is left of the oriental glories of Hope End in Herefordshire is an Eastern Palace with stables, built by Elizabeth Barrett Browning's father, Edward Moreton Barrett, between 1810 and 1815. He bought the estate in 1809, when Elizabeth was three, and immediately demolished the existing Queen Anne house, setting to work on wild flights of Islamic fancy. The house has gone, with its domes of glass and cast-iron, murals of Turkish views, door inlaid with mother-of-pearl, and minarets with spires and crescents; but the stables which echo all this strangeness are still there. Elizabeth's pony, Moses, had a minaret, and the yard is surrounded by great thick columns with flattened domes. Of the clock-tower, once like a ship in full sail with five spires, only the dome remains, with gaping holes; the clock, very unexpectedly, may be found in the courthouse of Brown's Town, Jamaica, where Edward Barrett grew up.

Shadwell Park

The archway into the stable-yard of Shadwell Park, near Thetford in Norfolk, was built in 1856–60 by Samuel Sanders Teulon, who according to Goodhart Rendel was 'the fiercest, ablest and most temerarious of Gothic adventurers'. Teulon had already rebuilt the local parish church of St Andrew's at Bettenham when Sir Robert Jacob Buxton commissioned him to enlarge his house and stable offices. Only fourteen years earlier, Edward Blore had rebuilt Shadwell for Sir John Jacob Buxton, and while Teulon's enlarging of the comfortable pseudo Tudor/Elizabethan house is in sympathy with Blore's design, his work is nevertheless startling and fantastic, high Victorian architecture at its boldest and most exhilarating. As Mark Girouard writes, Teulon's buildings are 'prickly, rocky, dramatic, assertive', they 'bristle with individuality', and 'anything striped, spiky, knobbly, notched, fungoid or wiry fascinated him'. His critics, as these wild proportions reared up all over the country, were many, those uncertain of their merits describing them as 'muscular'. The wealth and mixture of materials at Shadwell is delectable, with the rough flint and the smooth stone and slate. Brick is introduced in the stable court, pleasingly diaper patterned into the flint.

Through the arch, under the 'Tower of Babel' (as Sir Robert's mother, Lady Buxton, used to call this vast appendage to their house), is a highly elaborate flint courtyard, once again happily mingled with stone, above which rise Dutch and pointed gables, spires, and a medley of half-hipped, shallow and steep roofs. A Gothic niche sheltering a stone horse's head surrounded by chestnut leaves is carved above another arch into the stables.

Stone pheasants are 'hung' over the entrance archway, and to the left of the photograph, just visible, is the motto that soars up above the front door, carved into the elaborate layers of eight Gothic arches: 'UNLESS THE LORD BUILD THE HOUSE, THEY LABOUR IN VAIN THAT BUILD IT'.

Manderston

The stables at Manderston in Berwickshire were built for a King of the Turf, Sir James Miller, one of the great racehorse owners of his day, whose Rock Sand won the 'Triple Crown' (the Derby, the St Leger and the Two Thousand Guineas) in 1903.

They were designed in 1895 by the Scottish architect John Kinross, who was given a working budget of £20,000. Six years later, when commissioned to rebuild the house, he was told by Sir James that 'it really does not matter' how much it cost. The fortune had been founded by William Miller, trading with Russia in hemp and herrings. Honorary British Consul in St Petersburg, he was knighted by Gladstone in 1874. His eldest son died choking on a cherry-stone, and so the second son, James, inherited Manderston in 1887.

Kinross's stables are magnificent, but entirely restrained – four neo-classical ranges of grey stone around the main yard. A handsome, pedimented Doric arch leads you through, under carvings of a hunt in full cry and a great brass bell, into the paved court, which is laid out in a neat radial pattern of bricks set in grey stone. Directly opposite is another pediment over the arched doorway of the stalls. The loose-boxes and the coach-house face one another to the right and left.

Inside as out, the workmanship is of outstanding quality. The barrel-vaulted roof, the carved ventilators and the stalls are of teak, the posts and balls of solid brass. The names of the horses appear on marble tablets set into brass filigree frames above each stall. Like Miller and Manderston, they all begin with M: Mango, Malakoff, Magic, Monarch, Marsden, Mystery, Matchless, Margot, Milton, Mabel, Mercat, Maiden Erleigh, Monty and Milly. The floor is made of woodblocks, and the halters hanging on the polished brass balls are of soft white kid. The stables at Manderston have been claimed by *Horse and Hound* to be 'the finest ... in all the wide world'. They are still in use today.

Perhaps these glories would not exist if Sir James had delayed building by a year or two. He had failed to see the potential of the motor car, and soon found himself having to construct an immense 'motor house' for this new form of transport. Lined with ceramic tiles throughout, even in the working pits, it had marble inlays round all the taps and radiators.

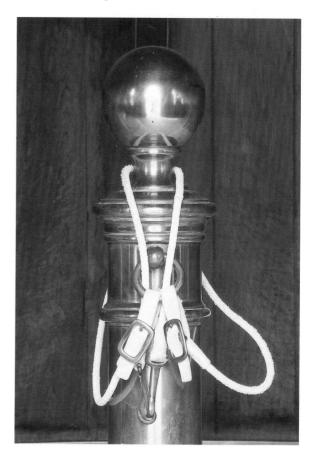

48

Swarkeston

The arena at Swarkeston in Derbyshire, thought by many to be for bull-baiting or deer-slaying, dates from 1630. Attributed to Robert Smythson, it was built for Sir John Harpur of Swarkeston Hall, a great house nearby which was demolished after the Civil War. The pavilion, in which the spectators would sit, had a fireplaced room upstairs, with the arched loggia beneath; both were sixteen by fourteen feet. One tower was for the staircase, and in the other was a small room, thought to be the 'garderobe'. The 'cuttle', or enclosure, with its shoulder-high stone wall, is almost square – sixty by seventy yards. The stonemason was Richard Shepherd, the cost £111 12s 4d.

It was common practice to drive deer into an enclosure and kill them at close range. Queen Elizabeth I had a 'delecate bowre' prepared for her by Lord Montequte at Cowdray in 1591, 'under which were her Highnesse musicians placed, and a crossbowe by a Nymphe, with sweet song, delivered to her hands, to shoote the deere, about some thirtie in number put into a paddock, of which number she killed three or four and the Countess of Kildare one. Then rode her Grace to Cowdray to dinner, and about six of the clocke in the evening, from a turret, sawe sixteen bucks ... pulled down with greyhounds.' Blood and gore were part of the ceremony, and it was customary to tread barefoot in the stomach of the slain deer, as it was thought to strengthen the sinews.

The sentiment behind bull-baiting was less barbarous, in that it was believed that the meat would be tenderised by the exercise and agitation of the bull. Butchers were legally obliged to bait their animals before slaughter.

Brighton

The stables at Brighton, designed by William Porden for the Prince of Wales between 1803 and 1808, were built years before the Pavilion and towered over the Prince's modest establishment, a farmhouse which had been enlarged for him by Henry Holland.

Influences from the east had started to infiltrate into the Prince's plans by 1801 with a scheme to add a Chinese façade to his villa, but this did not materialise, and the first oriental building of any size to be built in England was Porden's Indian temple for horses, modelled in its general plan on the Jami' Masjid in Delhi. The dome was inspired by the Halle au Blé, a cornmarket in Paris, and was huge, at eighty feet in diameter, only twenty feet short of the St Paul's dome. In 1804, when the building was finished, there was a general terror that as soon as the scaffolding was removed it would crash to the ground. Even Porden wrote to his daughter, 'The cupola is now on, and the workmen are swarming about it like jackdaws. The whole proves fully to expectation. The dome now supports itself, without assistance from the scaffolding, and has not yet fallen.'

There were forty-four stables, five coach-houses and two harness rooms in the great circle, all with their scallop-arched windows and doors. Upstairs were twenty bedrooms, leading off the arched balcony. The cost was enormous, thought to be at least £60,000 … and the Prince never paid his bills. Mr Sanders, who was in charge of the timber work, died a broken man, with £10,000 owed him.

The watercolour of the outside is by Humphrey Repton, from his folio of twelve views of Brighton, produced for the Prince in 1808. He describes with enthusiasm the 'stupendous and magnificent building which, by its lightness, its elegance, its boldness of construction and the symmetry of its proportions, does credit to both the genius of the artist and the good taste of his royal employer.' The interior is from John Nash's *Views of the Royal Pavilion* (1827).

Holland, Porden and Repton all drew up plans for the new Royal Palace, and James Wyatt submitted a scheme in 1813 but was killed before it could be realised. It was left to Nash to complete the oriental enclave in 1826.

Virginia Water

George IV's Fishing Temple at Virginia Water was a fashionable fancy begun in 1825 by Sir Jeffrey Wyatville (born Wyatt, his grand augmentation was sanctioned by the King when the first stone of his transformation of Windsor Castle was laid), and later lavishly decorated by Frederick Crace. Samuel Sanders Teulon's designs for the repairs and redecoration are shown here. The original estimate of some £3,000 bore no relation to the sumptuous demands made by the pleasure-seeking 'King-Fisher', as the satirists called him, and by 1828 over £15,000 had been spent. The Chinese Temple stood on the edge of Virginia Water, the 120-acre artificial lake made in 1750 for the Duke of Cumberland by Thomas Sandby.

There were originally two Chinese pavilions at Virginia Water: 'The Mandarin', built on a hulk which floated in the middle of the lake; the other, a cluster of three elaborately carved, trellis-worked octagon buildings with bell-like 'umbrellas' on their tall finials. The Mandarin was fantastical – forty feet long, with a scaled dragon painted the full length of its hull. Its 'mast', or finial, rose up as high again as its glass-walled room and was decorated with moons and a 'Chinese hat' hung with bells. The roof was striped, with dragons' heads swooping up off the edges. Banners and lanterns on posts stood on the deck, which was surrounded by a wooden, 'lozenged' balustrade of the same pattern as the glazing bars on the windows.

George IV's Fishing Temple was as elaborate, with its curving creatures around the finials and its bells hanging from the roof of the fishing balcony and from the mouths of the dragons on the fishscale tiled roof. It was described by Greville in 1830 as being 'beautifully ornamented with one large room and a dressing room on each side, the kitchen and offices are in a garden full of flowers, shut out from everything. Opposite is moored a large boat, in which a band used to play during dinner, and in the summer the late King dined there either in the house or in the tents.' The eight 'tents' were the little open 'Turkish' structures, with crescent moons on their central poles, that stood dotted about nearby. The pavilion, always in a state of poor repair, was demolished by the end of the century.

Monkey Island

Monkey Island, on the River Thames at Bray in Berkshire, became terra firma after the Great Fire, when barges carrying stone to London for the rebuilding of the City were loaded up with unwanted rubble on their return journeys to the Berkshire quarries. This was dumped on the islands along the Thames, raising them above the levels of flood danger and giving them a solid base on which to build.

When the Third Duke of Marlborough bought the island in the early 1700s, the fishing temple was already there, faced, as it is today, with hefty, rusticated blocks of wood simulating stone. He built another temple, and employed Adien de Clermont to paint his 'grotesque' scenes on the fishing house. De Clermont came to England from France in 1717. He was a Rococo figure, who

painted elegant monkeys besporting themselves in *scènes galantes*. 'Singerie', as it was known, was what he excelled in. He also painted a ceiling at Kirtlington Park in Oxfordshire, with graceful monkeys astride greyhounds, hunting the hare. At Bray, the monkeys shoot (one is cruelly killing a kingfisher), punt, angle and net fish, while one is harpooning a dolphin. There are two monkey 'beaters' putting up a snipe, another two carrying a basket full of eels and fish, and an otter with an eel in its mouth. In the central panel, two monkeys sail out to sea, serenaded by a third, blowing a conch. Embracing one another, they sit in a shell drawn by dolphins spouting water.

The doors in the room are tiny: the tallest person expected to pass through them would be only five foot four.

Studley Royal

The Fishing Tabernacles at Studley Royal in Yorkshire were built in 1727 by John Aislabie, Chancellor of the Exchequer at the time of the South Sea Bubble, during his forced retirement from Parliament. He had gone north to his estate, and was to devote twenty years to creating ornamental grounds, with pools – 'The Moon' and 'The Half Moon' – canals, cascades and lakes. He built two temples, of 'Piety' and 'Fame', a banqueting house, an octagonal tower, a grotto tunnel and these fishing houses. His gardener was William Fisher, and the stonemasons responsible for the fishing temples were Robert Doe, Richard Moor, John Simpson and Thomas Buck. No architect is recorded, and it would seem that Aislabie must have designed everything himself.

The balustraded dam, the fishing houses and the cascades divide the Studley Royal estate from the grounds of the Cistercian Fountains Abbey. One of the features of Aislabie's landscaping had been the 'Surprise View', when the vast abbey ruins suddenly appear between the trees. He had always wanted to buy the adjoining estate, and eventually his son William managed to do so, in 1768.

Beneath the fishing lodges are sluice tunnels. The windows to the sides opened for angling, which was mainly for trout, grayling and roach, the salmon strain having been killed off by the cascades.

Tendring

The mid-eighteenth-century temple for fishing
and coursing near Stoke-by-Nayland in Suffolk
stands in the grounds of what was once Tendring
Hall, and has been attributed to both Sir John
Soane and Sir Robert Taylor. In a single, elegantly
plastered room, with an overmantel which soars
almost to the ceiling, fishing could be viewed
across the water from one window, the glass of
which reaches down to the floor, and coursing
across the fields from the other, an enormous bay
taking up two-thirds of the north-facing wall.

John Soane built Tendring for Admiral Rowley
in 1764, and Humphrey Repton proposed plans
for the gardens with his 'before and after' water-
colours. But now everything has gone. The house
was demolished in the 1950s, and Repton's Red
Book has long since disappeared. Only the
Temple, as it is called, remains to give an idea of
the charms of the Admiral's life. Today it is a
sympathetically restored and converted private
house. The *oeil-de-boeuf* window beneath the
arch was designed by Sir Raymond Erith to admit
light into a little kitchen.

The canal is artificial and fed by springs. It is
set obliquely to the house, to give the illusion of
greater length from the saloon, and measures some
200 by 38 yards. It was originally stocked with
trout; now it is full of carp.

The kennels stood next to the Temple, the
hounds being kept for coursing on the flat Suffolk
countryside beyond.

Alresford

The Chinese fishing pavilion by the lake in what were once the grounds of Alresford Hall, Essex, is known as 'The Quarters', and stands in woods of the same name, said to originate from the Civil War when Cromwell's troops were quartered in the area. The pavilion was built *c.* 1765, when it appeared to be setting sail across the lake, with its little verandah hanging over the water. The bank was extended earlier this century.

An 'Estimate for the Building of the Chinese Temple for Colonel Redbow' survives, said to be in the handwriting of one Richard Woods and giving as £343 13s 4d the cost of evoking the East in Essex. 'Chinese' buildings had started to appear all over England by the 1750s. 'The Country wears a new face', enthused Horace Walpole, with 'a whimsical air of novelty that is most pleasing.' Alresford is sensibly and delicately restrained. Contemporary fancies involving wild profusions of bells and dragons have seldom survived, but we have an eighteenth-century description which gives some idea of the style: 'With Indian and Chinese subjects great Liberties may be taken, because Luxuriance of Fancy recommends their Productions more than Propriety, for there is often a Butterfly supporting an Elephant or Things equally absurd ... '.

John Constable painted the pavilion in 1816. His patron was General Isaac Redbow, who commissioned two pictures specifically so that the artist would have the means to marry his fiancée Maria Bicknell. Constable wrote to her in August 1816, 'I am to paint two small landscapes for the General; one in the park of the house and a beautiful piece of water; and another a wood, with a little fishing house where the young lady (who is the heroine of all these scenes) goes occasionally to angle.' The painting has gone to Melbourne, Australia.

There was another building on the site when Woods started work, and he incorporated it into the fabric of the temple. The room under the sliding Chinese roofs is octagonal, square in plan, with disguised cupboards for fishing tackle cutting off the corners.

In 1951–2 the building was extended to the south and converted into a house, without any loss of its charming character. Looking out through the windows, it seems that you have cast off from the moorings and, with the water all around, floated to the middle of the lake.

Netherby

A pink sandstone castle was built in the 1750s to guard salmon at Netherby in Cumbria. Coops formed part of a dam across the River Esk, which flows just behind the building. One in four of the stone waterways was blocked off, trapping the salmon, which cannot turn round. A door was dropped down behind them to secure their capture.

In 1783, a Border raid by some 200 armed and 'disorderly' men disbanded from the Duke of Beccleuch's regiment of 'South Fencibles' sought to right a wrong long suffered. They felt too many salmon were being stopped, and were determined to destroy both the dam and the coops. It had been attempted twice before, 'but had been repelled by the Netherby tenants with all the spirit of ancient times'. Hutchinson's *History of Cumberland* (1794) goes on to report that, 'As no person of property or weight took any part in this insurrection, some magistrates and gentlemen of the English side, by mild expostulations, settled the matter amicably.'

The salmon keeper lived upstairs in the castle, which in the early 1900s was occupied by a family of eight, who had pet owls sleeping on the end of each bed.

Southill

The fishing temple at Southill in Bedfordshire, built by Henry Holland between 1796 and 1800, was commissioned by Samuel Whitbread II, whose father had bought the house a year earlier for £85,000, asked for Holland's advice, and then died almost immediately. His great-grandfather had been 'the red-haired Captain' Whitbread, whom Cromwell always said he 'could never do without'. The Whitbreads were a local farming family whose fortune had been made with Samuel I's brewery, founded in 1742. He was the MP for Bedfordshire from 1762 to 1790, and it is said that it was he who drew Pitt's attention to the need for slave trade reform.

The house is reserved in style, and so is the temple, which can be seen across the lake to the north. It is reached by a simple stone bridge, which like the house and the fishing lodge is of perfect proportions.

The road takes you round to the back of the temple, which is a complete surprise. The front portico has been carried back, across the little building, and juts out over the path behind to provide a *porte-cochère* for the arriving carriages of fishing parties. The back walls are arcaded with great brick 'entrance and exit' arches, at right-angles to the buildings, across the path.

The front and back porticoes are each supported by four Tuscan columns, and those on the front, with the steps leading down to the lakeside, have the names of Samuel Whitbread's children carved into their bases. Inside is a feast of plasterwork which is totally at odds with the rest of the building: feathery Corinthian columns support three tiers of highly ornamental fluting and flowered friezing, while the ceiling is criss-crossed with bands of moulding halted at every angle by a huge plaster sunflower. 'Capability' Brown, Henry Holland's father-in-law, landscaped Southill in 1777, and it is thought that this plasterwork, and therefore the core of the fishing lodge, is part of his designs.

Holland himself was a man of immense wealth, who bought 100 acres of Chelsea in 1780 and laid out Sloane Street, Cadogan Place and Hans Place. He designed Claremont House, near Esher, for Lord Clive (of India) and built several additions to Woburn Abbey (q.v.), as well as being responsible for many and diverse buildings in London, including Battersea Bridge, the Drury Lane Theatre and the alteration of Carlton House.

The Stomach

Packwood

There are thirty beeboles in all at Packwood in Warwickshire, set in pairs into the seventeenth-century wall that divides the terrace from the remarkable yew garden, with its magnificent rows of giant trees said to represent the Sermon on the Mount – twelve 'Apostles', four 'Evangelists', and so on.

Straw skeps sheltered in the beeboles, made of 'clean unblighted rye-straw', as advised by William Cobbett in the early 1800s, or of 'wicker … made of privet, withy or hazell', as Charles Butler recommended in the early 1600s. Grasses, such as reeds and sedges, were also used. Previously, old crocks, little thatched stooks and 'penthouses' (sloping roofs) had protected the skep, or cow dung 'tempered with gravelly dust or sand or ashes' (Butler) had been daubed on. The beebole was the perfect alternative, a permanent niche where the skep could stand undisturbed. To thwart thieves, there was sometimes an iron bar locked across the wall.

Beeboles were considered a great convenience, and not at all a luxury. Homes from the most modest to the grandest would have them. Packwood is remarkable for the number that were built, and for their prominent position in such distinguished surroundings. They march along either side of a handsome eighteenth-century wrought-iron gate, with both walls ending in a gazebo. In one of these little buildings stands a fireplace with a horizontal fire which warmed the peach wall, encouraging a succulent harvest for the occupiers of the skeps.

63

Berthddu

This old photograph shows an unidentified castle for bees in Wales which used to stand at Berthddu, Llandidau, in Powys. The date is not known, but judging from the clothes of the top-hatted old gentleman and the lady hiding from the camera it stood in the mid-1800s. Behind the chair can be seen a straw skep, which seems just too big for the castle. Bees lived in real towers in Ireland. In a 1966 edition of *Beecraft* magazine, 'Historia' writes of turrets and towers forty and fifty feet high, built by the Cistercians in the twelfth century, and *c.* 1230 Nicholas de Verdon built, at Clonmore, County Louth, a stone skep ten feet square and almost fifty feet high.

Hartpury

The shelter for skeps at the Gloucestershire College of Agriculture, Hartpury, is the oldest and most distinguished beehouse in England, dating from before 1500. Twenty-eight hives fitted into the carved niches, and five more could stand under the arches on the ground. The whole building is enormous – thirty feet long, eight feet high, and built entirely of stone, most of it quarried from Caen in Normandy. Originally it stood at Minchinhampton Manor in Nailsworth, which had been granted to the Abbaye aux Dames by William the Conqueror and Queen Mathilda. For 500 years the dues and rents were paid to the Abbess, who must have wished to improve her estate in England with this strange and rare beehouse. The stonecaps and roof slabs are of Cleevehill Peagrit, the 'plates' of Purbeck stone. The crosses may well have been there to proclaim the God-given nature of the bee. Hilda Ransome in *The Sacred Bee* writes that in the classical world of northern Europe honey was thought to come from above, with the bee as the medium for bringing it to man.

In 1968, the Stroud branch of the Gloucestershire Beekeepers' Association dismantled this shelter in what had become the grounds of Nailsworth Police Station. It was discovered that the panels were held together with thick oak pegs and that the stones weighed a total of over five tons. A sealed plastic container was put for posterity into a cavity carved out of a pier. It holds an account of the rebuilding, with the names of all those who worked on it, a bottle of mead, some coins, both decimal and £.s.d., and a copy of the Gloucestershire Beekeepers' Association Year Book.

Hall Place

The central post of the ten-sided pavilion for bees at Hall Place (now the Berkshire College of Agriculture), near Hurley, is a tree-trunk, a rustic feature so often suggested by architects in their eighteenth- and nineteenth-century pattern books, and so seldom seen. It is turned upside down so that the buried branch stubs act as anchors, and from the bench which surrounds it the beekeeper could tend the hives from behind. The hives stood one at each window, in which there was an aperture that could be opened or closed. In the eaves and beneath the windows the bands of trellis cover panels of perforated zinc which allow the air to be constant and keep the hives draught-free. Good ventilation and an even temperature are essential for bees.

The exact date of this little building, with its Chinese lilt, is not known, but we have two clues. The roof timbers have been cut with a band-saw, which was not used in England before 1859; and the pavilion appears to have been built for movable frame hives, which were developed by the Rev. Langstroth in America in 1851, and not brought to England until 1862. Traces of an earlier beehouse found on the site suggest that the pavilion was built to celebrate the arrival of the new type of hive.

Attingham Park

The eighteenth-century latticework beehouse at Attingham Park in Shropshire had two shelves of hives, six on each, with arched openings allowing the bees to come and go. The point of beehouses was that you could manipulate the hives from behind, which was not possible with stone skeps, and so it would seem that these buildings owe their origin to the development of the wooden hive.

Beehouses, pretty little buildings in their own right, were usually attached to an estate rather than to individual houses, however prosperous, providing wax, honey and mead on a suitable scale. They reached the height of their popularity in the late eighteenth or early nineteenth century.

Bee Bole in Gloucestershire

Kit Williams, author of *Masquerade* and *The Bee on the Comb*, built his bee garden in 1983–4, transforming a quarter of an acre of hillside into a series of dry-stone walls, terraces and paths, with a pottery hive, wooden hives, bees in skeps and a beehouse for humans from which to enjoy the garden.

Trees, herbs and flowers have been planted around the colonies. The needs of the bees have dictated every detail: to have paths in front of the hives, for instance, might interfere with the departing 'flight path', and a screen of espalier trees has been planted to encourage the bees to rise up immediately into the open. It also provides limbs on which the returning swarm can land within reach of the reclaiming beekeeper.

All the herbs and flowers have been chosen with care. The nectar provides carbohydrate, the pollen protein. Different plants have different coloured pollen, and as bees store selectively multicoloured combs can be produced – pockets of black from poppies, turquoise from willowherb.

Another harvest gathered by bees is propolis, a resinous glue collected from tree buds which they use to repair the cracks in their hives or, more sinister, to seal intruding snails in their shells.

The Centenary hive is made of pottery. Kit Williams based its shape on the comb made by wild bees – the form of the strongest arch known. The house for humans is a reconstruction of a seventeenth-century beehouse, which is circular, with a conical roof held up by two elm-trunk pillars. Instead of the niches or shelves for hives, there is a circular bench and one bee bole.

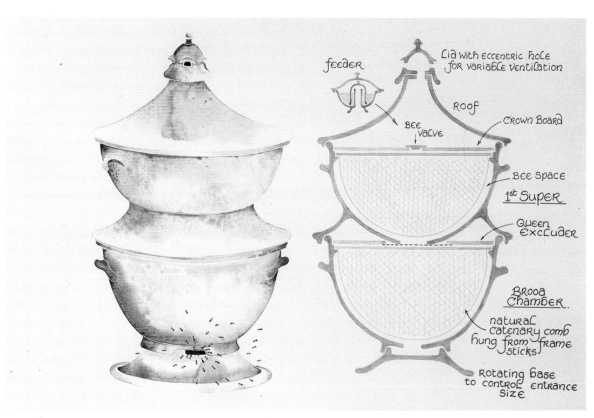

Biddick Beehives

The beehives in the apiary garden at Biddick Hall in County Durham were designed by my father in the 1970s, with the four little 'Chinese Chippendale' buildings placed formally in a square of quarters of lavender and gravel, surrounded by tiny hedges and pyramids of box.

When my parents moved to Biddick in the 1940s, they found the garden wrecked, the ground churned up by anti-aircraft guns and Nissen huts, a formal lake no longer in existence, replaced by a nineteenth-century tennis court. They dug wide borders and planted beech hedges which have now grown tall, creating a splendid 'room' to greet you when you have paraded past the clipped may trees on the lawn. Within, sixteen rosebeds are united by a formal planting of clipped yews and juniper sky-rockets (the nearest English equivalent to a cypress) about a twisting stone sundial.

Once through this outdoor chamber, another gateway of beech leads you into the apiary garden, with tunnels of overhanging weeping elm leading off to the right and left.

On either side of the main garden lie the orchard and the Italian and vegetable gardens. Long greenhouses run the full length of one wall, and a grass avenue of roses the other. The Italian Garden was also made by my father in the early 1970s. Through a brick arched gateway you come upon a round and fountained pond, which heads the straight and beautiful line of a brick path, thickly overhung with 'old-fashioned' roses. There are two square 'rooms' and another round garden, with a stone rose-window embedded into the earth and planted with blue lobelia to give the effect of stained glass. A row of juniper sky-rockets marches up to a rose-covered temple.

The whole idea was to create gardens where formality was softened by informal planting, the informality returned again to order by a succession of relating paths and avenues. Everywhere are walls of the prettiest coloured bricks.

Swallowfield Park

The 'skirt' roofs of the dovecote and cattle shelter at Swallowfield Park in Berkshire would appear, from a plan of the estate, to date from 1844, but the main octagonal building is much earlier, presumably contemporary with the house which was built by William Talman in 1689–91 for the Earl of Clarendon.

Inside the dovecote, brick pillars stand at each angle, with the 535 brick nests set in rows, five abreast, between them. The main beam to support the potence post still survives. Outside, the walls have recently been restored. The angles had been worn away by the cattle, which had softened them all the way round, up to the height of their backs.

Biddick Dovecote

A grassed beech avenue sweeps down to a fountain and the dovecote beyond, which stands in the middle of a plantation of mixed wood, avenues forming a radial pattern of which this temple for doves is the pivot. Nothing is known about the little building, which was bought from Crowther of Sion Lodge in the early 1960s.

Launtley Court

The 1673 post and truss dovecote of Launtley Court in Hereford predates the farmhouse by a year, which suggests that the owners prudently arranged their 'larder' first, and near to hand, providing sustenance while the building work went on. Herefordshire is full of these little black-and-white dovehouses: Bidney Farm, with its curving timber framing; Kings Pyon, with a lantern; and the Butthouse, with its carved beams and gables – all within a few miles of each other.

Hurley Dovecote

The dovecote at Hurley in Berkshire, dating from 1307, seems to be the earliest in England. The little building is eighty feet in circumference, with walls three feet thick. Outside, four buttresses, to the north, south, east and west, climb up to the cone-shaped roof with its square cupola. The jambs and lintel were built at a later date: '1642 C.R.' (Carolus Rex) is visible above the door. Inside, everything is still in perfect working order, with a 'potence' – a central wooden post with arms that radiate out to the walls – still revolving with ease around the 600 chalk nests. With the ladder set against an arm, you can climb to any height, and by pushing against the walls propel yourself round in the complete circle. The potence was an early importation from France, and to support it the Norman dovecote with its circular opening to the skies had to be altered. Norman dovecotes were round, sturdy and solid, with stone walls, some three to four feet thick, and a central opening in their vaulted roofs.

The dovecote at Garway, in Hereford, is Hurley's rival in age and has all the characteristics of an earlier pigeonhouse, yet it is thought to have been built almost twenty years after Hurley.

Friarscroft in Dunbar

The grotesquely altered fifteenth-century dove-cote on Friarscroft in Dunbar was once part of the Abbey founded in 1218 by the Fifth Earl of Dunbar. The building now stands alone and peculiar, with the wedge-shaped addition crammed onto its gables. Inside, an ordinary ladder was used to reach the nests. A small potence supported by a beam was added in the top.

It was the Normans who decreed that no one other than the Church and the landowners should benefit from the pigeonry, and no one else did. One case, of 1577, records that a tenant was ordered to demolish his newly built dovecote.

As a medieval pharmacopoeia, the dovecote had a role of importance. *The Ornithology of Francis Willoughby* of 1678 tells us that, 'A live pigeon cut along the back bone, and clapt hot upon the head, mitigates fierce humours and discusses melancholy sadness ... For the vital parts of the pigeon still remaining in the hot flesh and blood, do, through the pores of the skin insinuate themselves into the blood of the sick person now dispirited and ready to stagnate, and induing it with new life and vigour, enable it to perform its soleumn and necessary circuits.' Dr Salmon, in his *Seplasium or The Complete English Physician* of 1693, includes a prescription 'of the powder of the dung of pigeons beaten and sifted 2 oz; of Bear's Grease 4 oz and pepper in powder 1 oz; oil of cumin $\frac{1}{2}$ oz'.

Phantassie

The dovecote at Phantassie, a farm at East Linton in Lothian, is curiously primitive in form. The horseshoe-shaped roof slants up northwards, protecting the flight-holes from the gales, and is sunk below the level of the wall, so providing a sheltered parade-ground for the doves. The 'beehive' bulge, with walls four feet thick and sixty in circumference, is encircled with two billet-mould friezes. Inside are 544 nests with fixed ladders, all in an immaculate state of repair.

Attempting to entice birds from your neighbour's cote became a common practice, with the most delectable baits described. It was suggested that, with their houses perfumed with frankincense and sage, their food sprinkled with red wine and cumin, and their feathers with myrrh, the doves' sweetness of breath would prove irresistible to the neighbouring flocks. Barley, millet, cumin, honey, old loam, mortar and muskadell boiled together, made into a 'stone' and set in the middle of the cote was another decoy, as was boiled thistle-root and herrings. The accounts of Jesus College, Cambridge, in 1651 have descriptions of 'Roasted Dog with Cumin', and 'Baked Cat with Cumin Seed' was also considered an excellent recipe for decoy. There is never a word on the morality of such preparations, only straightforward and robust advice on how to steal your neighbour's birds.

Antony House

The circular dovecote at Antony in Cornwall was restored, and a new potence installed, in 1982–3, by the Manpower Services Commission under the supervision of the National Trust. Antony House is attributed to James Gibbs, and was built between 1710 and 1721, replacing the Tudor or earlier 'poor home of my ancestors', as it was described by Richard Carew who lived there from 1564 to 1643. He built a 'fishful' pond (a tidal pond) and pilchard cellars at Portwinkle. The dovecote, which holds 300 nests, predates the house, but it is not known by how long.

Rathfarnham

The 1742 'Halls Barn' and the cone-shaped dovecote built by one Major Hall at Rathfarnham in Dublin once formed part of the estate of Whitehall, a pretty pedimented house. Now they stand in a neat bungalow garden near an icecream factory. Major Hall must have modelled these curious forms on the Wonderful Barn and the dovecotes at Castletown, built by 'Speaker' Connolly, who owned Rathfarnham Castle nearby. A plate of 1795 shows the dovecote without its little dome. The barn had two rooms, each with a fireplace, and a third tiny box at the top, all reached by the outside winding stairway.

Cliveden

The pepper-pot dovecote at Cliveden in Buckinghamshire is attributed to Henry Clutton, who built the dramatically extravagant clocktower in 1861. The two look at each other across the forecourt of Charles Barry's restrained house, totally at odds with its elegance and cocking a wonderful snook at its neo-classicism. Clutton went on working for another ten years at Cliveden – first for the Duke and Duchess of Sutherland (for whom the present house was built), then for the Duke of Westminster, who bought Cliveden in 1867. The urned walls stand parallel to the drive, adding grandeur to the approach.

Exton Park

The dovecote at Exton Park in Rutland dates from the mid-eighteenth century and was built when these little buildings were on the wane, their popularity impaired by the growing awareness of how much damage the birds could do to the crops.

It was the turnip and the swede that doomed the dovecote. In the mid-seventeenth century there were thought to be as many as 26,000 in England, allowing some thirty-five million birds daily to swoop on and plunder the crops. They were the luxurious living larders of the Lords of the Manor, landowners and all ecclesiastics until in the eighteenth century the rootcrop was established as winter food for livestock, and the pigeon was no longer the only animal that could be kept alive during the cold months.

This majestic arrangement at Exton, for sheltering livestock as well as doves, was built for the Fifth or the Sixth Earl of Gainsborough, and was probably seen as an eyecatcher from the old Hall, which was burned down in 1810 (the ruins still stand, to the east of the church, looking down over the park). The new Hall was built in 1850 and stands directly to the right of the dovecote. There is the prettiest fishing temple at Exton, castellated and arched, with quatrefoil windows and openwork pinnacles which seem to be floating lightly on the water's edge.

Pittencrieff Glen

The Romans were the first recorded pigeon-keepers, and wrote copiously on how it should be done: 'the whole building should be whitewashed', advised Varro, 'because this kind of bird generally prefers the colour', with 'smooth walls inside and out to prevent the entry of "noxious animals".' Pliny the Elder wrote of the chastity of pigeons: 'Promiscuous intercourse is a thing unknown. Although habiting a domicile in common with others, they will none of them violate the laws of conjugal fidelity, nor will one desert its nest unless it is a widow or a widower.' Columella wrote of a particular venom in the teeth of human beings which as well as tarnishing the metal in mirrors, would kill a young pigeon if vigorously bitten. He advised the hanging of earthenware pots in which young hawks were left to die, 'which secures the affection of the bird for the place, that it may never leave it.'

Pittencrieff Glen, Dunfermline, was given to the town by Andrew Carnegie. The dovecote, with its Gothic doorway, Greek cross arrow-slit window, and quatrefoil decoration and castellations, has all the appearance of a miniature castle. The nesting boxes were made of wood, and the birds went in and out through the cupola.

Willington Manor

Willington Manor, in Bedfordshire, was built between 1529 and 1545. The dovecote was added in the 1530s by Sir John Gostwick, who was both Master of the Horse to Cardinal Wolsey and Treasurer of the First Fruits and Tenths under Henry VIII. Sir John's mother acted as foster-mother to the King, who held a council at Willington in the 1540s. The dovecote was built of stone brought from the priories of Bedford and Newnham (demolished at that time) and was divided into two, with space for 1,500 birds.

Five buildings surrounded it, one, a training-school for horses, large enough to allow a coach and six to practise inside.

Upper Harlestone

The fifteenth-century dovecote at Upper Harlestone in Northamptonshire has smoothly rounded walls of local sand and ironstone about fifteen feet high and three feet thick. The circular roof, with its octagonal lantern, is clad with local Collyweston slates and shelters 400 nests. The string course with its downwards slope looks particularly vermin-proof. The Dovecote Laundry was closed in 1974 but its blue tin sign remains.

Minster Lovell

The dovecote at Minster Lovell in Oxfordshire, thought to date from the fifteenth century, was built to serve the old Hall of 1431–2 that stood amidst the trees on the banks of the River Windrush. The Hall was demolished in 1747, but the dovecote still survives, meticulously restored with its tiers of stone nesting boxes and wooden rafters supporting the conical roof.

The Hall, and probably its dovecote too, was built by William, the Seventh Lord Lovell, whose grandson lost the estate to the Crown after his support of Richard III at the Battle of Bosworth. The fate of this last Lovell remained a mystery until in the early eighteenth century, when a new chimney was being built into the old Hall, a grim solution presented itself: 'there was discovered a large vault or room underground, in which was the entire skeleton of a man, as having been sitting at a table, which was before him with a book, paper, pen &c., and in another part of the room lay a cap, all much mouldered and decayed, which the family and others judged to be this Lord Lovell, whose exit hath hitherto been so uncertain.' So relates Peck's 'Historical Pieces', attached to his *Memoirs of Oliver Cromwell* (1740).

Castletown

The dovecote is one of two smaller versions of the Wonderful Barn at Castletown, the Palladian pile in County Kildare built by William 'Speaker' Connolly. The house was begun in 1722, to designs by Alessandro Galilei, and was unfinished when Connolly died in 1729. His widow lived on and built two extraordinary eyecatchers: the Connolly Folly, an obelisk supported by tiers of eight arches, which stands, clearly closing the vista, two miles to the back of the house; and the Wonderful Barn, a working building on a farm but standing at the end of another view from Castletown and built to honour its position. A castellated cone with an outside circular staircase, it has a stone plaque above the entrance with the inscription: '1743 EXECUT'D BY JOHN GLINN' (the second 'n' is tiny, squashed into the space of a full stop). Presumably he built the dovecotes as well. All three are of the same dressed stone and curious cone-shaped form.

Corby Castle

In 1748, Phillip Howard built on the red sandstone façade to the Tudor dovecote at Corby Castle in Cumbria, as a memorial to his Italian fiancée, who had died. 'A QUELLA CHI LO MERITA' is inscribed along the frieze above the pillar capitals. There are few flight-holes, just five to the right and six on the back. Inside the potence is still intact, with two ladders connected by an oblong platform, giving access to the 750 brick nesting boxes.

Corby is full of curiosities. There are two more temples, with pediments of sea-horses and Apollo, and in the garden a great cascade flows down through statuary – giants, putti with a goat, nymphs and dolphins, and Cerberus dogs pouring water from their mouths, flanking a creature with stone fangs. The deep red stone of the dovecote is everywhere.

Saltoun House

The dovecote at Saltoun House in Lothian is attributed to Robert Burn, who castellated and turreted the house in 1803, only to have all his work obliterated by his son William's wholesale medievalisation fourteen years later. A deep and dramatic ravine separates the two buildings.

Mertoun

The four-tiered, 'tun-bellied' dovecote of Mertoun in Roxburghshire dates from 1576. It is a great trek from the house – you would have had to walk a mile there and back for the eggs. As so often in Scotland, where enormous value was put on the 'columbarium', the walls are thick and the door small and low to protect the inhabitants from the serious but constant crime of dovecote-breaking.

Megginch Castle

Captain Robert Drummond built the Gothic stableyard and dovecote at Megginch Castle in Perthshire in 1806–7. The Chinese air of the lilting roof was probably influenced by Drummond's botanical journeys to Macao, which he made in the East Indiaman *The General Elliot*, in which his elder brother had brought back the first double red camellia to England in 1794. A model of the ship, the first copper-bottomed vessel in the East India fleet, acts as weathervane.

In the stable-yard stands a great oak tree, planted in 1815 in memory of Captain Drummond by his sister and brother, with a halfpenny placed in the roots for luck:

92

Vauxhall Farm at Tong

A fox is caught escaping from the 'Egyptian Aviary', the henhouse of Vauxhall Farm at Tong in Shropshire, and the only remaining building of a collection that had in England no equal in eccentricity.

A Mr George Durant was responsible. Having grown up in the domed and pinnacled Moorish house which his father had built after demolishing a medieval palace at Tong, he set to work with filial zest on improvements of his own. The gateway, part of his extraordinary scheme, had ten-foot high pyramids set on ten-foot high gate piers and flanked on either side by an ornamental castellated wall, along which a stone rope rose and fell, ending in a tasselled loop around the pier. On this wall, Durant built a pulpit from which he would preach to passers-by. In the dark pink stone wall were a mass of carvings, of a snail, a bat and a pierced heart, a skep of bees, artichokes, a snake, a bat and a butterfly.

The henhouse was also used as a dovecote. Once in sight of the gateway, it is now cut off from what used to be the estate by the embankmented M54. Twenty feet high, in yellow brick with dark blue vitrified quoins, it carried inscriptions, of which there is now no trace, reading 'SCRATCH BEFORE YOU PECK' and 'TEACH YOUR GRANNY'. The sandstone carvings too have gone, of a cat carrying a kitten and labelled 'TRANSPORTATION' and a swan amongst bullrushes. A bas-relief of a cockerel was inscribed with the date of the building: 'EGYPTIAN AVIARY 1842'.

Two more fancies – a pyramid for pigs inscribed 'TO PLEASE THE PIGS' and a Gothic cowshed inscribed 'RANDZ DE VACHE' (*ranz-des-vaches*, a Swiss-French herdsmen's song) – are at Acorn Cottage, Bishops Wood, Staffordshire.

Blaise Hamlet

In 1810, a Quaker banker, John Scandrett Harford, commissioned John Nash to build houses for his retired estate workers at Blaise Hamlet, Bristol, and into one of the gables of these 'rustic' cottages, built of rubble, some with weatherboarding and plaster facing, are built these quarters for doves.

The nine cottages present a pinnacle of the picturesque – every one different, and every one a delight. They bulge and soar in every direction. Gabled, hipped and half-hipped and pyramidal roofs built variously of pantiles, stone slate and thatch, bear chimneys rising up in giant Elizabethan proportions, diamond-shaped, polygonal and circular, with patterned encrustations of terracotta.

Shadwell Park

A tame bear lived for some time in the game larder at Shadwell Park, near Thetford in Norfolk, part of Samuel Sanders Teulon's sensationally extravagant plans for Sir Robert Jacob Buxton's house, built between 1856 and 1860.

Every kind of architectural exuberance forms the skyline: as well as the dovecote-like lantern of the game larder, there are the two spires of the stable arches, stepped and Dutch gables, ornamental stone and brick chimneys galore, a round and a square tower on the house, and innumerable stone spikes and finials.

Arthurs O'on at Penicuik

This fair dome where suit is paid
By blaste of bugle free.
                    Walter Scott

Whoever owns the lands at Penicuik pays no rent to the Crown so long as they stand on the Buckstone and blow three blasts on the horn when the Royal Hunt is out on Boroughmuir.

'Arthurs O'on', the dovecote built in 1766 by Sir James Clerk in the stables of Penicuik House, Mid Lothian, is a replica of the Roman temple of Victory which stood by the Antonine wall in Stirlingshire. The temple was pulled down by Sir James's father, Sir John Clerk, in 1743, during extensive improvements at Penicuik. He always vowed that he would reconstruct the temple, but it was left to his son to do so. Inside, the nests are reached by a two-ladder potence still in smooth working order.

Rosebery House

The spired dovecote was built over the 'pend' in the steading of Rosebery House, Lothian. The spiked gate pier in the foreground belonged to the Gothic house (now demolished) built for the Fourth Earl of Rosebery in 1812–16, by William Atkinson. The bowfronted plinths with their sharp points are all that remain, leading you happily across the road to the spired steading, which is of an earlier date, built for the Third Earl in about 1805.

Welbeck Abbey: Cowsheds

The three cowsheds at Welbeck Abbey have a lightness the other buildings, all rather lumpen neo-Tudor, lack. On the right was the milking parlour, the other two sheds containing individual stalls for the cattle and one continuous feeding trough.

The Duke of Portland was a strange recluse who lived a good deal of the time underground – or otherwise in rooms with no furniture at all save a 'convenience' in the corner – and considered it good aesthetic management for his tenants and animals to do the same. He instructed that the clergy, the doctor and his tenants should not recognise him when he passed, and issued all his workmen with donkeys and umbrellas. He built forty-one 'large ornamental lodges', some of them with underground stables, white-tiled tunnels leading from the house to the cows, calves, chickens, pigs and perhaps a donkey. A pierced quatrefoil cast-iron grille allowed the animals air. The lodges were identical from the front and back, with porches and great dummy chimneys.

Poultry-house

The poultry house at Welbeck Abbey in Nottingham was built by the Fifth Duke of Portland in 1857, and is part of what amounts to a stately village for animals built between 1857 and 1878. The plans for the poultry house show a squat spire instead of the dome and are signed C. C. and A. Dunnet. Two cottages flank the building, one for the poulterer, one for the dairyman (the dairy which stood nearby has been demolished). The hens lived in the middle, with rows of nesting and feeding boxes separated by long passages and with a wooden, arcaded 'covered way' so that they could have an airing – or they could be let out to roam on the grass surrounding an ornamental fountain. Near the cottage stood a little annexe for parrots and canaries. Four stone birds stood on the corner pillars of the poultry house; a turkey, a grebe and a stork remain. It was emptied of fowl in 1982. This poultry yard would have provided the 'perpetual chicken', as it was called by Lady Ottoline Morrell, whose stepbrother inherited Welbeck in 1878.

Lightholer

Timothy Lightholer's 'Design for a Sheep Cote to be built on a hill which seen from a Genteel House forms an agreeable object' appeared in the *Gentleman's and Farmer's Architect* in 1762. It contained 'a great variety of Useful and Genteel Designs ... Pinery, Peach, Hot and Green Houses, with the Fire-Wall, Tan Pit etc. particularly described ... Cow Houses, Stables, Sheepcots ... ' There are twenty-five copper-plate engravings, one with plans to Gothicise a haystack! Three illustrations are shown, one with an unadorned haystack, the other two with crumbling ruins disguising it. The farmhouse and barn are of the same Gothic, with and without arrowslits and castellations.

Lightholer also proposed to build Gothic 'out offices', to house oxen, cows, horses, hounds and spaniels, and classical cow and ox sheds with arcaded wings.

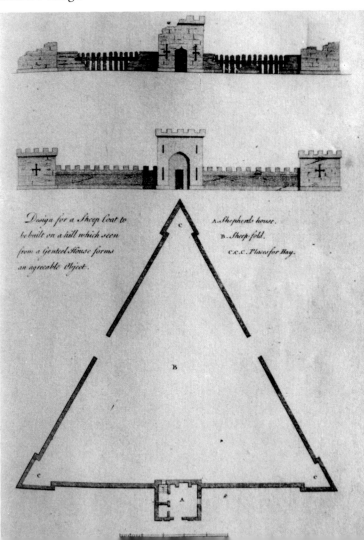

Design for a Sheep Coat to be built on a hill which seen from a Genteel House forms an agreeable Object.

A. Shepherds house.
B. Sheep-fold.
c.c.c. Places for Hay.

Port Eliot

Sir John Soane's cowshed was part of extensive alterations to the house and estate at Port Eliot in Cornwall, commissioned by the Second Lord Eliot in 1804, when Soane had been working for some years on his houses in London and Gloucestershire.

Lord Eliot, a man of action and taste, had already done much of the landscaping himself, as well as reclaiming a tidal creek. Soane was to remodel the house with a vast circular room, and build heavily machicolated Gothic stables, a dairy and this ingenious cow-house. Beneath the eaves, what seems to be a fluted frieze is in fact a ventilating system, operated by pulling a knob to slide a panel aside, thus opening the 'flutes'.

Elihu Burritt discovered the joy of clotted cream, at Port Eliot, in 1864: 'that most delectable of luxuries ... I remember meeting with an old musty volume many years ago, containing a learned disquisition in Latin on the question whether the butter which Abraham placed before the angels was really butter or this very cream.'

Soane's Pattern Book

Sir John Soane's dairy in the 'Moresque' style appears in his pattern book of 1778, produced when he was only twenty-five and advertised, at 'six shillings sewed', as by John Soan, the 'e' of distinction yet to be added. He had worked for George Dance for two years from the age of fifteen, and then moved on to Henry Holland, who was in partnership with 'Capability' Brown. In 1776 he won the Royal Academy's gold medal for architecture, with plans that so impressed George III that he was awarded the King's travelling studentship.

Soane was responsible for many elegant animal buildings, and at Wimpole in Cambridgeshire he designed a thatched farm, rustic and grand, on an enormous scale. Also at Wimpole, he built these wooden nesting-boxes, as well as 'capital piggeries' and deer-pens, for Lord Hardwick, and for Lord Clarendon in Watford a wooden chicken-house.

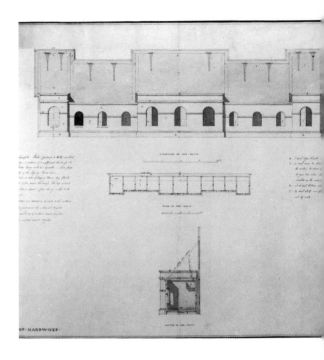

The Royal Dairy at Windsor

The Royal Dairy at Windsor is the best, the prettiest, the most enchanting dairy in England, a glistening jewel of nineteenth-century decoration. The building is in the process of being restored, and only John Thomas's design can be shown. The gleam of ceramics, with their violent and vivid colours, must be imagined.

Tiny china oranges, their leaves entwined with blue and white ribbons, weave about the walls and are repeated, double the size, in plaster on the ceiling. Ceramic roundels of Queen Victoria, Prince Albert and their children are supported by seahorses, and V and A medallions by dolphins. There are majolica tableaus of babies enjoying seasonal pastimes – skating, sheep-shearing, gathering the harvest and dancing around the maypole.

Harebells and hawthorn arch in the stained-glass windows, while the Tudor Rose bears the thistle and shamrock leaves on its stems. There are two Minton fountains, one in the form of a merman, the other of a mermaid, both supported by cranes, arum lilies, waterlilies and bullrushes.

Behind all this flamboyant opulence is Prince Albert's sound practicality. The windows are double-glazed throughout to maintain an even temperature. The dairy is air-conditioned with a paddle, which draws any fumes from the oil lighting through the pierced ceiling tiles and out through the 'air tower'. The width of the doors allows for the yoke and buckets. And beneath the floor a rabbit warren of pipes flow with water to keep everything cool.

Fort Putnam

The cowhouse of Fort Putnam, a farm of Greystoke Castle in Cumberland, with its stone petal coronets, was built *c.* 1778 by the Eleventh Duke of Norfolk – an ardent Whig and a supporter of the rebel forces in the American War of Independence – in order to spite his neighbour and enemy the Tory Earl of Lonsdale, with whom he was on fiery terms. He built four farms: 'Jefferson', 'Bunkers Hill', 'Fort Putnam' and a fourth with a spire, reputedly for a tenant whose religion deemed a church not to be necessary. (Bunkers Hill was the first battle won towards Independence, and General Israel 'Puffing' Putnam was prominent in the campaign.)

Lord Lonsdale and the Duke were constant rivals, politically standing as Whig and Tory candidates for Carlisle, and at home raising building for building on their neighbouring estates. They make a startling picture of two highly eccentric and unedifying men. Lord Lonsdale's temper was such that he was judged by many to be mad. He was known as 'Old Thunder', was perpetually picking quarrels that would end in duels, never paid his debts, and kept his mistress's head in a glass case after her death. The Duke was as colourful. 'Nature, which cast him in her coarsest mould, had not bestowed on him any of the external insignia of high descent. His person, large, muscular, and clumsy, was destitute of grace or dignity … He might indeed have been mistaken for a grazier or a butcher … At a time when men of every description wore hair-powder and a queue, he had the courage to cut his hair short, and to renounce powder' (*Wraxall's Posthumous Memoirs*). He was clever, hard-working and well liked, but was drunk most of the time, spending many an evening 'under the host's mahogany'. He seldom washed, being with regard to cleanliness 'negligent to so great a degree that … his servants were accustomed to avail themselves of his fits of intoxication for the purpose of washing him.' He over-ate to such an extent that 'he seemed incapable of passing through a door of ordinary dimensions.'

Rousham

The cowshed at Rousham in Oxfordshire stands at the end of a 'finger' of the gardens, with the cows living on one side, where the open fields begin, and the humans enjoying the gardenscape from the other. It was built by William Kent as part of his 'picturesque' layout of the grounds in the 1730s.

The building is castellated to the front and back. There is a seat in an arched and turreted alcove which is both to be looked at and to be looked from. A Palladian gateway is built into the wall of the park, to the left, and vistas flanked by urns sweep you off into the gardens beyond.

Its inmate now is a Longhorn bull, Longhorns being among England's oldest breeds, now classified as rare. They were bred at Rousham between 1910 and 1927, and again from 1971, when there were only ten other breeders in the country. There are now 140 members of the Longhorn Cattle Society, but still only 750 beasts. Rousham has three bulls and twenty-five 'suckler cows'. They are huge, very hardy, living out all the winter, and with their long, lean carcases make excellent beef. Despite their magnificent and fearsome appearance, they are docile and easily handled, with a reputation for being good mothers.

Woburn Dairy

The Chinese Dairy at Woburn in Bedfordshire was built by Henry Holland while he worked on the house for the Fifth Duke of Bedford between 1787 and 1802. Humphrey Repton had exotic plans for surrounding the building with a Chinese garden. 'Of all the countries which Europeans have discovered, the Chinese are the only people whose prudence, or cunning, or jealousy prevents a cordial intercourse with them; it will therefore be an additional source of novelty to form the banks of this pool after the manner of Chinese landscape.' He thought the diary had a 'gay singularity', and that its appearance justified 'the novelty of an attempt to extend the character of the building to the scenery in which it is placed', the view towards the dairy being 'riante', that from the dairy 'trieste'.

The covered walk (p. 112) that curves round from the end of the pond once swept on to the house some quarter of a mile away. Prince Pückler Muskau described walking down it in 1826: 'An unbroken arcade clothed with roses and climbing plants ... over the arcade are partly chambers, partly the prettiest little greenhouses. One of them contains nothing but heaths, hundreds of which, in full blow, present the loveliest picture, endlessly multiplied by walls of mirror.' The walkway continued with a 'lofty Palm House' and passed the statue gallery with 'very beautiful pillars from Italy', thence on and on through 'an interminable plantation' until it reached the dairy.

In the Prince's day the dairy was decorated inside with 'a profusion of white marble and coloured glasses', 'hundreds of large dishes and bowls of Chinese and Japanese porcelain of every form and colour filled with new milk and cream' lined the walls, and in the centre stood a fountain. Now it is a dimly lit delicacy of colours and forms, with painted and fashioned 'bamboo', stained glass, and marble on the ceiling, walls and floor.

Robin Hood's Bay

The Grecian Temple for pigs at Fyling Hall, near Robin Hood's Bay in North Yorkshire, is the most splendidly appointed animal house of all. The portico and pillars are of wood, the base stone, brought by horse-drawn sledge from a local quarry half a mile away. It was built *c.* 1883 by Squire Barry of Fyling Hall, an inveterate traveller who was constantly returning from abroad with some new plant, tree or architectural plan. Just such an enthusiasm was the temple, with its pillars, portico, tapering Egyptian windows, fluted frieze and acanthus-leaf drainpipe head all being concocted for pigs.

Three men took two years to build the sty. In 1948 Matthew Hart, a stonemason from Scunthorpe, recalled the frustrations of Squire Barry's incessant changes of mind as to what the style should be. A previous owner of the temple saw the Squire in 1932, and described him as 'a very courteous old man who used to wear what we called a Daily Mail Hat – a top hat cut short – that was very popular at the time.'

Plaw's Dovecote and Sheepfold

The Monastic Farm from John Plaw's pattern book of 1797 was 'calculated to ornament an extensive domain, and to unite the useful with the agreeable ... The entrance gates, with the turrets and towers, have a monastery-like appearance: these embosomed with stately trees give an air of antiquity, consequence and grandeur.' There were over thirty-eight plates in this *Ferme ornée or Rural Improvements calculated for landscape and picturesque effects*.

The Fold Yard from the *Ferme ornée* was a proposal for an enclosure with a wall built of rough old materials to give a monastic character. 'This enclosure will be very useful to fold sheep in, in severe weather ... or for cattle and horses needing extra feed.'

Three designs for a cattleshed also appear, in classical, Gothic or grotesque – 'whichever character may accord with the adjoining buildings, or whichever shall best please the fancy of the builder.' The 'grotesque' could commemorate 'some favourite animal for past services ... The skull of a horse may be placed over a mural tablet, where may be recorded the feats of that noble animal, and the water trough may represent the sarcophagus.' Plaw avoids Eastern influences, but otherwise all architectural avenues are explored. A rustic cattleshed is shown, with gnarled Doric pillars and Gothic doors, built around a tree which sprouts out of its thatched roof.

Plaw was one of the many architects who were to produce pattern books in the late eighteenth and early nineteenth century. Robert Adam and John Soane, as well as Joseph Gandy, Timothy Lightholer, Thomas Wright, Robert Lugar and many others, sallied forth into this venturesome and tolerant field of rural architecture. You could be as fanciful as you liked, enhancing the landscape with your towers and spires without fear of defying tradition, or of complaints from the inhabitants about inconveniences caused by flights of architectural fancy.

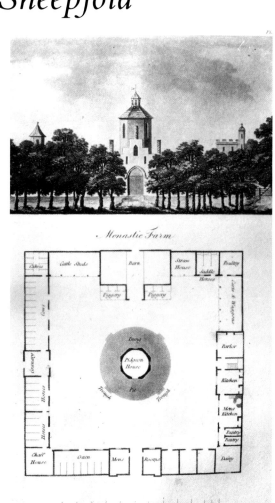

Monastic Farm

A Fold Yard.

Manderston Dairy

The model dairy at Manderston in Berwickshire was designed for Sir James Miller by the Scots architect John Kinross in 1900 as part of their prodigious building project which had begun in 1894 and ended in 1906.

After he had completed the stables (q.v.), Kinross was instructed to rebuild the Home Farm in the Scottish Baronial style, with houses for the dairymen and head gardener, and the mock Border keep for the dairy and tea-room, which lead into Gothic cloisters surrounding a courtyard with a fountain. Stately progress can be made through the cloisters from the milking parlour at one end to the dairy at the other. This handsome vaulted room is made from marble and alabaster from seven countries, carved by French and Italian artisans. The ceiling boss of a dairymaid milking a cow is known to weigh half a ton. She sits under a tree, with her hair in a bun and her ribboned straw hat lying by the stool. When it was originally hauled into place, Sir James saw to his horror that she was milking on the wrong side, and it had to come down and be carved all over again.

Above the dairy there is a little oak-panelled room for sipping tea. Everything now is as neat as it was then, immaculate order preserved throughout. When Sir James progressed round his estate, he would ring a bell as he entered the garden, the stables and the dairy, to warn of his arrival.

Belvoir

The dairy at Belvoir is thought to have been designed by the Duchess of Rutland and James Wyatt as they worked on the remodelling of the castle between 1801 and 1813. The Duchess was the driving force behind the plan to rebuild the sombre seventeenth-century block into the enormous 'Mediaeval' castle that looms over the vale of Belvoir today, visible for miles around. While taking an active part in the work at Belvoir, she was also drawing up architectural schemes for Hyde Park Corner, York House, a Thameside quarry, and many and various improvements to London and its parks.

At Belvoir, the Duchess gardened and land-scaped extensively in the already dramatic terrain, and at the end of her favourite walk she built her dairy. 'This building is indeed a beautiful object at various distances, and in various directions', wrote the Rev. Irvin Eller in 1841. 'Viewed from the garden gate ... it appears the terminal point of a suburb avenue ... it might be mistaken for the mansion of a small ornamental farm.' The Duchess was a serious agriculturist, who would have applied herself assiduously to the workings of her dairy, which is given an honourable mention by John Claudius Loudon, the great exponent of agricultural efficiency, in his *Encyclopaedia of Cottage, Farm and Villa Architecture* of 1833.

Meols

In 1948 Mr Roger Fleetwood Hesketh applied for planning consent to make alterations to his house at Meols in Lancashire. He found these could be allowed only for animals, and so designed this 'shippon' for his Jersey herd. Employing Mr Rimmer, a local builder, Roger Hesketh supervised the day-to-day progress. Work was begun in 1950 and finished in 1952 (the date can be seen on the central keystone).

The cowshed was a triumph. It is both pleasing to the eye and agriculturally efficient. The bulls were housed to the left, with the calving pen be-hind them, and the calves lived on the right, with the dairy beyond. The cow 'standings' for milking lead through from the dairy, across the back of the building. There is space in front of the central door for tractors to bring in the fodder, which was then stored on the first floor above the lunette.

As this part of England is predominantly arable country, the herd was sold in 1965. The cowshed is now a joiners' workshop, the cartwheels and barrows for Liverpool Market making most sympathetic tenants.

Badminton

The cowhouse, dovecotes and barn of Castle Barn and the pigsty and stable of Swangrove House, both at Badminton in Gloucestershire, are by Thomas Wright of Durham, a mathematician and astronomer of distinction who was at the peak of his powers when the desertion and death of many of his patrons forced him to turn to architectural and landscape design.

'I am sorry the stars have used you ill', wrote William Cowper, who had a cynical view of those in the fashionable world who had at first lauded and then abandoned his friend. He mocked that Wright's celestial erudition had been but 'laying a lane before them which concentrated all their greatness into an atom … Now you lay before them their own greatness, and what is really the fruit of your genius shall hereafter be shown as the contrivance and art of the great proprietor.'

Wright worked at Badminton for thirty-six years, producing for the 'great proprietors' Charles, Fourth Duke of Beaufort, and then Henry, the Fifth Duke, a quantity of fancifully castellated and rustic buildings, as well as a temple on a hill with a pedimented grotto below and a thatched hermit's cell.

He built several castellated lodges and a Root House, thatched and Gothic with an arcade of contorted tree-trunks, and he designed a Chinese façade for Swangrove, a 'maison de plaisance' with two pavilions built on the edge of the park. The castellated pigsty and stable stands discreetly away from the house.

Castle Barn can be seen looming up like a great Keep, a mile away, across the fields. The two towers were dovecotes, and the central crow-stepped block was the cowhouse and barn.

Gandy's Piggery

The design for this Entrance Gate and Double Lodge for pigs, poultry and their keepers was proposed by Joseph Gandy, the distressingly unfulfilled pupil of both Wyatt and Soane. In his pattern book, *The Rural Architect* of 1805, Gandy suggested all manner of rather spartan designs, with a hint of Italianate form. The two or three lodge arrangements stand out in their idiosyncrasy, but sadly neither the pyramids for pigs, nor all the Italianate 'bungalows' (as they appear to be), were ever to see the light of day. The book is a poor example of Gandy's glory, which lay in his imagination and draughtsmanship. In Rome, when he was only twenty-four, he won the Pope's medal for architecture, and for years was to execute wonderful designs and drawings for Sir John Soane – often, sad to say, with too much of the credit going to Soane. Very few of Gandy's plans were realised in stone, bricks and mortar. The *Dictionary of National Biography* describes him as having had 'too odd and impracticable a nature to ensure prosperity ... his life was one of poverty and disappointment, ending, according to some accounts, in insanity.'

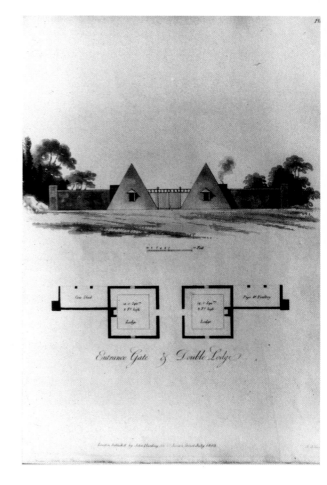

Sway Pigsties

The spirit of Sir Christopher Wren built the Moorish concrete pigsties at Sway in Hampshire, or so claimed Judge Peterson, late High Court Judge of Calcutta, who erected several farm buildings and two slender towers of concrete in 1879. According to Barbara Jones, in *Follies and Grottoes* (1953), Peterson wrote an autobiography recording his 'working directions' from the spirit of Wren, 'who was impatient to see concrete take its rightful place as a building material.' This tantalising book has vanished.

The tallest tower, 218 feet high and 22 feet square, had 330 steps leading up to a little Indian polygonal lantern, roofed, and with Gothic windows, one above the other, set into elongated Gothic recesses. It is said that Peterson wanted to be buried beneath the tower, and that a smaller, less Eastern version was for his wife's remains.

All the buildings are in rough aggregate 'shuttered' concrete (set into wooden frames rather than reinforced). As an advertisement for its excellence they fail, since the towers have had to be reinforced and the farm buildings are of interest rather than beauty. A grim warning of concrete, and high-rise concrete at that, they appear exotic and strange in the Hampshire countryside.

Culzean Castle

Robert Adam produced his plans for the home farm, with its barns, pigsties, calf-pens, cattleshed, ox-house and stables, in 1775, for the Earl of Cassillis at Culzean Castle, Ayr. Three years later, John Bulley, the farm manager, was still waiting for work to begin. 'I have not a proper farm yard, nor a house or shed for feeding cattle, or for the convenience of raising so much dung as might be made; but these things will come in course. Lord Cassillis has an extensive and very commodious plan of offices, which he intends to build soon.'

It was the age of 'Improvement', when the architect in charge of the house might well be asked to design the farm buildings as well. Adam's plans were of striking originality. The cross bars of four T-shaped buildings form a central square and arched courtyard, with large turreted arches across the corners. The long barns at right-angles have crowstepped gables, surmounted by crosses. They stand looming high over the sea, as does the castle 400 yards away.

In 1971–3, the buildings were completely restored under the architect Geoffrey Jarvis of the Boys Jarvis Partnership, the National Trust for Scotland and the Countryside Commission for Scotland. The project was so successful that in 1975 it won the European Architectural Heritage Award. The original sandstone was re-used whenever possible, together with a variety of new stones, to give the effect of the colour changing so admired by Adam. All the roofs were retiled in West Highland slate. It is a triumphant renovation.

To make the oyster pool in the rocks below the castle, stone slabs were embedded into the rocky outcrop to form a tank in which locally caught oysters were trapped alive and delectable for fresh consumption. Marks round the tops of the stones are still visible where a metal mesh was attached to prevent them from being washed away by the tide. The tidal action clarified any oysters that may have been contaminated.

The little Gothic duck-house on the island of Swan Pond, a thirteen-acre lake in the grounds of the castle, was built in the nineteenth century as a nesting place convenient for collecting the eggs. Culzean's only natural stream, the Hogsturn Burn, is held back to form the lake. Robert Lugar, who was building the pheasantry that stands on its shores (q.v.), described it as 'entirely surrounded by plantations and wood, the surface of the water enlivened by swans and various kinds of fowl, together with wild fowl which frequent it in considerable numbers.' And so it is today, with over 600 ducks enjoying the company of the world and his wife out for day trips from Glasgow.

Farnborough Hall

The eighteenth-century game larder at Farn-borough Hall in Warwickshire is thought to be the work of Sanderson Miller, with the stonemason William Hiones of Warwick. Five elegant little structures were built, all complimenting each other: three along a great elevated terrace, with the game larder reached by a little path as you return to the house. The fifth, a pentagon summer-house with a balcony, has gone. The terrace itself, dating from the 1730s, gave a taste of the 'Picturesque' to come – a grassed and curving walk above the great plain of Warwickshire, with the pavilion, a temple, an obelisk, and semi-circular grass 'platforms' to project you out into the countryside.

Decoration

Biddick: Dog Niches Birdcage

The dog niches in the dining room at Biddick Hall were built by my mother and father in the early 1950s as part of their improvements to the 1718 enclosed peel tower. As a Jacobean house, attached to the tower, Biddick was bought by Sir William Lambton in 1610, who steadily dissipated his fortune by having twenty-nine children by his two wives and by taking the King's side in the Civil War. In the early eighteenth century Freville Lambton had the tower clad in elegant pink-red bricks, tapering Ionic pilasters, with great bulging capitals, corner-stones and a central pediment.

My father and mother moved into the house in 1948 to find the Jacobean wing was about to fall down. E. M. Lawson and Partners were employed on its rebuilding, and the results are entirely satisfactory, with a long wing of eighteenth-century bricks, pyramidal finials and a large wooden dovecote built onto the end wall. The dining room was refashioned at this same time by Trenwith Wills, with a plasterwork ceiling and the china cupboards with their dog niches. The dogs' names are incised on hanging brass plaques. Hops of Hereford (born in Hereford at Harvest time) is posing, sitting absolutely still for a full minute exposure. A long-haired dachshund, she belongs to my son, Huckleberry Harrod.

'In form, cages may be procured from that of a common fig-box to a miniature representation of the Crystal Palace at Sydenham. I have seen cages of almost every imaginable pattern, representing cottages, abbeys, castles, cathedrals and palaces, with fine fluted columns, porticos with pediments, stained glass windows etc., rich and varied in design, and in every known style of architecture including Gothic, Doric and Ionic, and displaying great taste and marvellous mechanical skill' (Robert Wallace, *The Canary Bird*, 1893).

The eighteenth-century birdcage at Biddick Hall is built of beechwood with inlaid bands of ebony, rosewood and yew. It stands, with its legs, about five feet high.

Proper little houses, these cages became popular in the early eighteenth century and remained so until the twentieth. Often the work of cabinet-makers, and even designed by architects, these little Chinese pagodas, Gothic churches and castles, and classical palaces were usually made of wood with little iron bars at the 'windows'.

Birds have been kept in ornamental cages since classical times. Trapped and wretched, linnets, larks, nightingales, cuckoos, chaffinches and starlings were considered ideal companions for ladies from the fourteenth century to the sixteenth. Popinjays (the early name for parrots) were considered more suitable for men and were often allowed to fly free. Sir Thomas More had twelve uncaged parrots swooping about his house. Canaries, too, were kept in the 'singing cages', little domed or lanterned structures attached to a richly woven cord and hung low in the room for their occupants to be admired; when hauled up to the ceiling, the bird would immediately burst into song. Vile practices to encourage bird song included tongues cut for a better trill; blinding was also said to improve the tone, as well as making the bird more docile. By the eighteenth century objectors to this appalling cruelty were beginning to make themselves heard.

Thomas Wright's Aviary

'The Elevation and Plan of an Ornithon, or Arbour of the Aviary Kind, chiefly contrived for the Reception of Singing and other beautiful Birds' by Thomas Wright of Durham is from his *Universal Architecture* of 1758, of which Book I is devoted to 'Six Original Designs of ARBOURS', while Book II has 'Six Original Designs of GROTTOS'. The aviary was with the arbours ... 'as derived from "ARBOR", a Tree, the principal Material made use of in the Execution of these rude DESIGNS'. He describes 'The Manner of Executing this Design ... with the rugged trunks of Oak, the more fantastical and robust the better, the Architrave or Eve-band is of the same unhewn Material, and supports a like rude Cornice, in some Degree reduced to Order and Design, with large and prominent regular Nobs instead of Modillions; the roof is thatched, and of a Roman Pitch, with a Palladian Projection ... on the inside it may be fitted up with Ivy-Flakes and Moss, or otherwise with the roughest Bark of Oak, variegated and comparted with Knots, yet so as to appear all of one Mass growing together by the Consent of Nature'.

Book II has a drawing of an arched and pedimented rock-work cave entrance, designed chiefly for the use and ornament of a menagerie – 'the most Agreeable Accompanyment with-out will be Oak, Elm, Beech &c mix'd with Holly, Ivy, Mountain Ash, Chestnut and Thorn'. There is also a design for a 'rustic' folly, with a 'ruin' growing 'abandoned' out of the back. Little round, domed projections stand either side of the roughly hewn stone arch over the Gothic door.

Most bizarre of all is the 'Grotto of the Antique Ruin Kind, supposed to have been the Abode of an Anchorite', a castle of considerable complexity with a façade 124 feet wide. There are arrow slits, niches, and quatrefoil recesses in various stages of decay. The castellations have already crumbled, but all the stone 'eyebrows' over the windows and doors remain intact. The walls are pitted with 'weathering', and the two round towers that flank the façade are only half standing. Wright wrote that 'it may be finished in the Grotesque Manner' and that 'This Sort of Building can't be too Conspicuous'. If you did not want a hermit living in an enormous Gothic Chinoiserie Castle on your lawn, it could easily be formed into a 'magnificent Cold Bath'.

The Salute Birdcage

Based on the Church of Santa Maria della Salute in Venice, the Salute Birdcage was designed by Quinlan Terry in 1980. It is now in Australia, but the architect's drawings can be shown, two of the twenty-four that had to be produced to give all the complexities of the design. There are two great domes, the main one balustraded and supported from below by twelve scrolled buttresses on which are prancing brass cherubs. Both the domes and the two *campanili* have lofty open lanterns.

There are seven porticos, with brass capitals on their Corinthian columns. The size of the cage was determined by these capitals, which are available from catalogues, and while the geometry of the proportions of Santa Maria della Salute has been kept, the architectural details are simplified.

The structure of the cage is all of limewood, including the three-sided sweep of the sixteen steps and the rusticated base. The wire and mesh is all of stainless steel. With its panelled mahogany pedestal, it stands ten feet high.

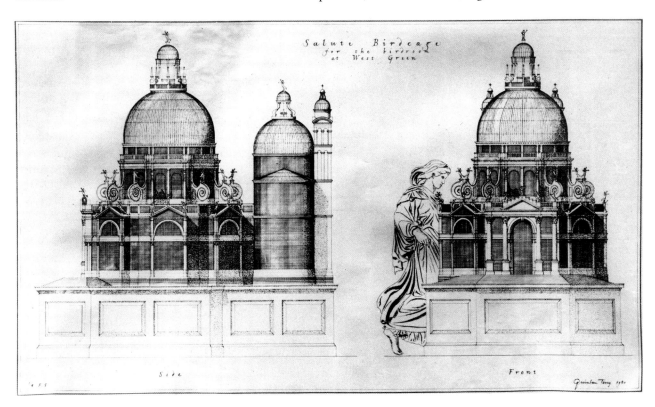

Salute Birdcage
for the birdroom
at West Green

Side

Front

Quinlan Terry 1980

Birdcages from Ireland

The first birdcage (*above*) from County Wicklow dates from the late eighteenth or early nineteenth century. It is wooden, painted glossy dark green and has two fretwork gables and a dome. The feeding troughs are of basketwork and the clock face is enamel; the little Gothic 'windows' are stuck onto the iron bars. Often cages of this period, with their latticework, fretwork and finials taking up a Chinese or Indian line, would be made entirely of wood, and William Cowper wrote a poem, 'On the death of Mrs Thockmorton's Bullfinch', about just such a flimsy home:

> Well-latticed – but the grate, alas!
> Not rough with wire of steel or brass,
> For Bully's plumage sake,
> But smooth with wands from Ouse's side.

The cage was gnawed by a rat, whose 'honours of his ebon poll were brighter than the sleekest mole', and poor Bully was devoured.

The second cage (*below*) from County Wicklow is dense and uncomfortable for its inmates. Its date is not known, but from all contemporary descriptions it would seem to be of the late seventeenth century, when rectangular cages were popular and wood was being used as much as metal, especially with upright corner posts. Nell Gwyn's birdcage of 1670 for her 'white sparrows' (canaries), which still survives, is the same size and shape, with oak barley-sugar corner posts and cross bars. There is a heavily carved band of wood around the base and a curving openwork pediment. Sticking out to one side is a bay which would project from the window when the cage was placed upon the sill.

Charles I was a great bird-lover, and Birdcage Walk was named after the site of his great aviaries in London. He managed to train a starling, and James I tamed a kingfisher.

Beckley Park

The 1749 castle for birds at Beckley Park in Oxfordshire is an exceptionally elegant but rather grimly enclosed architectural cage. Usually the back 'wall' would be made up of iron bars, giving more light and a feeling of greater space to the occupants, but here the birds would have only their sixteen Gothic windows to peer from.

Beckley Park is a rare survival – a hunting lodge of the 1540s, one room deep, surrounded by two moats, on the edge of Otmoor. Its atmosphere is of the past, pure, untouched and magical. Lord Williams of Thame who built the house might have kept his birds in far greater opulence; in the mid-1500s silver cages set with jewels were not uncommon, sometimes with real birds, sometimes with stuffed and jewelled imitations. But the eighteenth century produced the most elegant collection, with Chippendale and other cabinet-makers working away on these miniature buildings. Lantern-shaped cages, popular for hundreds of years, were still very much in use, now often to be found with their own stands inlaid with ivory and mother-of-pearl. Lantern cages of Sheffield plate are illustrated in the pattern books of the early 1800s. The German Prince Pückler Muskau wrote of a more prudent display in 1827: 'You know the English have stamped the day [Sunday] with a death like character; dancing, music and singing are forbitten; Indeed, the severely pious hang their canary birds in some remote corners, that no voice or song may offend their ears during the holy hours.'

Windsor

The aviary and poultry farm at Frogmore were built in 1845 by C. R. Stanley as one of the many improvements to the pleasure grounds of Windsor Castle begun by Prince Albert in 1840, the kennels for the Queen's pet dogs being another. Two lead dogs, 'Boz' (a Skye terrier) and 'Boy' (a dachshund), sit outside the dairy (beyond the aviary) today.

The American consul in Birmingham from 1863 to 1869, Elihu Burritt, known as the 'Learned Blacksmith' from the years he served as a blacksmith's apprentice, described 'this happified convention' in 1864. 'It gives the most elegant and comfortable housing to almost every kind of feathered biped known to ornithology … The large basin in front of the Aviary, with the fountain playing in the centre, is the very elysium of spoon-bills of every name, shape and size, ranging from the stateliest swan to the little tufted duckling trailing its shadow across the water, as if he had caught it at a dive and was afraid he would lose it. It is a constitutional monarchy of birds, in happy, and perhaps instinctive, harmony with the British Constitution. The royal family, the different orders of aristocracy, the peers, commons and plebs all seem to have been taught their places and prerogatives, and to move on together pleasantly like a well-regulated human society, of the European pattern.'

Woburn Abbey

Humphrey Repton designed the aviary at Woburn Abbey in 1804–5 for the Fifth Duke of Bedford. He also planned a large extent of pleasure garden, including a kangaroo enclosure, an American and a Chinese Garden and the menagerie, to be linked to the aviary. The designs were for a double-sided entrance – grandly pedimented Anthemion Doric from the menagerie into the aviary, Gothic rusticity in the form of a great semi-circular bower from the aviary into the menagerie. Repton wrote that he wanted the entrance gates to be in character with each species. Prince Pückler Muskau visited in 1826: 'The fourth or fifth attendant awaited us ... and showed us first several gay-plumed parrots and other rare birds ... As we walked out upon the open space our Papageno whistled, and in an instant the air was literally darkened around us by flights of pigeons, chickens and heaven knows what birds. Out of every bush started gold and silver, pied and common, pheasants; and from the little lake a black swan galloped heavily forward, expressing his strong desire for food in tones like those of a fretful child.'

Waddesdon

The aviary at Waddesdon in Buckinghamshire was built by Baron Ferdinand de Rothschild in 1889. He bought the estate in 1874 and set to work on levelling Lodge Hill, where the house and gardens now stand. The stones for this 'Renaissance' house were brought from Bath, hauled half-way up the hill by a little railway, and then pulled by a team of Percheron horses imported from Normandy for the job. Baron Ferdinand was brought up in Frankfurt-am-Main, where his mother had built a great aviary, and his sister, Baroness Adolph, was to do the same, at Pregny, near Geneva.

The house, by Hippolyte Alexandre Gabriel Walter Destailleur, and the gardens, by Laine, were both designed by Frenchmen, as might well have been this delicately grand pavilion for birds. Restored in 1960–6, it is still in use today, unmodernised except for the hospital and kitchens at the back, and considered perfect from an agricultural point of view. It houses 340 birds of eighty different species – macaws, toucans, toucanettes, aracaris, glossy starlings, and Rothschild grackles. At the back of each flight cage, built into the wall, is a glass-fronted 'internal shelter'. In most aviaries the public can peer in on all sides, but Mr Ian Hodgkiss, the keeper at Waddesdon, is sure that this causes strain to the birds and inhibits their breeding potential.

The water flowing from a fountain in each aviary is gravity fed from a tank on a hill nearby. The central grotto, of rocks and draping greenery, has a fountain with an eighteenth-century Italian marble figure of Minerva, military trophies and two marble tritons. On either side is an arched bay, with a seventeenth-century Italian triton in one and his companion, a young nereid, in the other.

Castle Ashby

The menagerie at Castle Ashby was built between 1764 and 1767 by Lancelot 'Capability' Brown, as part of his work for the Seventh and Eighth Earls of Northampton. Robert Adam met the Seventh Earl in Padua in 1767, and two years later was called in to draw up a grand design for a 'Pleasure Ground, Kitchen Garden ... small Park for Deer [and] Court of Stables'. Nothing appears to have been built, and it is thought that Adam's only contribution to Castle Ashby was a modest helping hand towards the design of the menagerie. Oddly, a temple on the same site is drawn into Adam's plans, but not Capability Brown's later ones.

The Eighth Earl succeeded his brother in 1763, when Brown's work was two years underway; it was to go on for another eleven. He destroyed all the formality of the terraced and walled gardens and the avenues, and wove meandering paths through the new landscape, complete with ha-ha. He enlarged the ponds and stews, and built a classical dairy, an ice-house and two bridges as well as the columned menagerie. He was delighted with the beauty of it all – 'Thames, Thames, thou wilt never forgive me', he cried one day when surveying its perfection from Terracotta Bridge, apologising for having eclipsed the glory of the Thames Valley! He was able to buy Fenstanton Manor from Lord Northampton in 1767 at a reduced price. He had given the Earl 'Taste in exchange for it'.

The Eighth Earl was an extravagant man, who never paid his bills and was an inveterate gambler. He was finally ruined, together with his neighbour Lord Halifax from Horton (q.v.), by his outlandish expenditure on the 'spendthrift election' of 1708: between them, they spent £160,000, with £6,000 for ribbons alone. Horton was sold, and Lord Northampton was forced to sell the contents both of Castle Ashby and of Compton Wynyates, his house in Warwickshire. The catalogue of creatures for sale in the menagerie survives – a few animals and a great quantity of birds.

Raskelf

The 'Pinfold' at Raskelf in the North Riding of Yorkshire is one of the few remaining in the country. From the Middle Ages until the late nineteenth century, these little enclosures were to be found in small towns and villages all over England. They were built as pounds (pound-folds) for stray and trespassing cattle, which would be locked up in the custody of the Pinder or Pinman until they were redeemed by their owners. This brick castle is thought to date from the late eighteenth century; it was restored by the Raskelf Parish Council in 1971.

'Pinfolds' were for animals, 'lock-ups' for men, and at Hunmanby, in the East Riding, they survive side by side, a circular stone pinfold next to a miniature brick prison dated 1834, with two cells, tiny barred windows and studded doors. 'The lock-up was used to house temporarily those who had erred and strayed like lost sheep; the pound was for four-footed creatures who had done the same', wrote the Rev. Bernard T. Croft in *Country Life* (19 July 1973).

Cabbage Castle

Charles Lamb (known as Charlie) decided in 1823, when he was seven, to create the Kingdom of Winnipeg for his guinea-pigs. It was built, observed, tended, and its history recorded, over many years, in eight miniature green and red leather volumes. 'The History of Winnipeg, from the foundation to the present time by Royal Command' was a chivalrous tale, copiously illustrated with guinea-pigs in armour, on and with coats of arms, in battles and castles, and as Kings, Queens, Princes, Princesses and Knights. A map showed the main walled city, six pyramid tombs, a columned monument, and the cities of Farai and Lelia.

Cabbage Castle, as this grand hutch was called, stood on its own, with flags flying. It was built by the estate carpenter at Beauport in Sussex, and by the 1830s the 'peeks' it housed had multiplied into hundreds. The original King Geeny and Queen Cavia had 'two blameless cheeldren', Limpy and Loidowiskea, and then 'pore Cavy, dear Cavia' died of consumption. Loidowiskea, now Queen, bore her father four children, seven more guinea-pigs arrived in the Kingdom, and the story began, written in Lamb's quaint hand: plagues of 'dusyintery', then consumption, carried off many of the bucks, does and 'cheeldren', Charlie lamented, 'and thus did ten thousand griefs happen to the Winnipegs'. The 'Rarribuns' (rabbits) were their troublesome neighbours, although they appear as arms-bearers along with the guinea-pigs. 'At their Zenith ... whenever there was panionium in came those gaulking ambassadors, jumping into all the hutches, breaking dishes, spilling corn, eating all the cabbage, drinking or washing in all the water, and bullying the inhabitants ... these horrid pests.'

Guinea Pig Castle Beauport 27 June ½ part 8 evening

The Jungle

'The Jungle' where Samuel Russell Collett kept his zoo, at Eagle in Lincolnshire, dating from *c*. 1820, is constructed of roughly formed burnt bricks, with Gothic windows and doors crammed into its gnarled façade. A Major General Loft visited the building in 1826 and described it as 'tasty and handsome', 'grotesque but not inelegant'. Of the animals he wrote that 'several Deer of different Kinds are kept here, the American Axis, which has produced a Breed with the Does; there are also several very fine kangaroos, a Male and a Female Buffalo (I think) and their young calf'. There were also several 'very fine gold pheasants' and a 'great number of gold and silver fish'.

Menageries were popular in the nineteenth century, private, public and travelling, with such figures as George Wombell, who lies buried under a stone lion at Highgate Cemetery, touring the land with their caravans of wild beasts. Prince Pückler Muskau saw such a spectacle at Nottingham in 1827, with 'Two Bengal tigers of enormous size ... so perfectly tame that even ladies and children were allowed to enter their cage ... A remarkable animal was the horned horse, or Nyl Ghau, from the Himalaya mountains ... in some respects very strangely formed.'

Wotton House

The temple for terrapins at Wotton House in Surrey stands in a little wooded enclave in what is thought to be the first Italian garden in England, created by the seventeenth-century diarist John Evelyn. It was much altered in the nineteenth century, but the terraced artificial hill and a temple remain as they were, heralds of gardening fashions to come.

Evelyn wrote *Silva*, the earliest authoritative work on arboriculture, and planted trees with zeal, as well as diverting waterways at Wotton, which he described with pride in the first pages of his diary: 'It has rising grounds, meadows, woods and water, in abundance ... I should speake much of the gardens, fountains and groves that adorne it, were they not as generally known to be amongst ... the most magnificent that England afforded, and which indeed gave one of the first examples of that elegancy so much in vogue and follow'd in the managing of their waters, and other ornaments of that nature.'

The terrapin temple was built between 1820 and 1830, either by George Evelyn or by his son William John, who was inordinately fond of animals. Helen Evelyn writes of them in her *History of the Evelyn Family* (1915): there were Indian cattle, chameleons, a vulture, and kangaroos 'let loose on Leith Hill, where they flourished for years until gradually exterminated by ruthless individuals'.

The terrapin house is in a sadly ruinous state, standing gauntly tall in its surroundings. There is a black and white, marble-floored Ionic portico, with niches, on and in which fragments of statuary still remain. Above, there was once a wooden pedimented 'summer-house', from which visitors would watch terrapins sporting in the pool below. The pool was fed by one of the tributaries of the Tillingbourne river.

Brighton

In 1806 Humphrey Repton produced a folio of twelve watercolours, among them an aviary, as designs for the Prince Regent's Pavilion at Brighton. The Prince was still living in the Marine Pavilion, a modest farmhouse enlarged by Henry Holland in 1787. The enormous Indian stables were added by William Porden in 1804, and Repton was now suggesting improvements of his own. The end in view, which had been denied to both Holland and Porden, was the plum job of building the new Pavilion itself. The water-colours show the scene 'before' and 'after', over-lapping flaps giving the view as it was at the time and lifting to show the trees and houses swept away and replaced by the elegantly positioned and planted improvements. A pheasantry and dove-cote were also included.

The aviary and pheasantry were both inspired by, if not directly copied from, Thomas and William Daniell's aquatints of 'oriental scenery' published between 1795 and 1808. Uncle and nephew, the Daniells had gone to Calcutta in 1786 and for six years had drawn and painted Hindu and Islamic architecture all over India. The aviary is drawn from one of the Hindu temples at Bindrabund, where, most suitably for Brighton, Krishna is said to have frolicked with milkmaids and to have stolen their clothes while they were bathing.

Another of the delights of this pleasure ground was a covered arcade, glazed in winter, open in summer, down which the Prince could stroll to his stables. It led through an orangery, a fifty-foot long hothouse, past the pheasantry and the aviary, and (to the right in the watercolour) through another Daniell-inspired building, the Hindu temple at Fort of Rotas, Bihar. At one point along the route, Repton advised that there should be an orchestra playing.

The Prince was delighted with all the plans: 'Mr Repton, I consider the whole of this work as perfect, and will have every part of it carried out into immediate execution; not a little shall be altered.' Nine years later, the folio was discovered to be still at the engravers. The Prince had never looked at it again.

Horton

The menagerie at Horton in Northampton combines an eyecatcher, a banqueting house, and a zoo built by Thomas Wright of Durham in the 1750s for Lord Halifax. This delightful little building, so small and yet grand in its perfect classical detail and proportions, was one of the many follies built to enhance the views from Horton, the Halifax house nearby, which was demolished between the wars.

The central block of the menagerie, with its split pediment and richly rusticated windows, was the banqueting hall. It has a magnificent array of plasterwork (recently restored) by Thomas Roberts of Oxford, with signs of the Zodiac, Father Time, Apollo and the Four Winds in curving deep relief on the ceiling, and Acanthus scrolls, cornucopias, a violin (of plaster, but strung with catgut), drums, books and all manner of glories bulging down the walls.

In 1763 Horace Walpole recorded seeing 'many basons of gold fish … several curious birds and beasts … Raccoons that breed there much … two hogs from Havannah with navels on their backs … two uncommon Martins … a kind of Ermine', as well as two eagles, two tigers, storks and 'doves from Guadaloupe … with blue heads and a milk white streak crossing their cheeks.' Four of the original six gold-fish 'basons' survive, perfectly round, and evenly spaced behind the building.

By 1975 the menagerie was derelict and in a dismal state of disrepair. It was used by soldiers during the war and had been abused over the years by vandals. The half-dome was gone, as were the pavilion roofs; the arches had been concreted up; and over half the plasterwork had disappeared. In the last ten years, Gervais Jackson-Stops and the artist and designer Christopher Hobbs have, with meticulous care, completely restored this little temple.

Culzean Castle

The monkey-house at Culzean was built for the Earl of Culzean and Cassillis, Marquess of Ailsa, in the early nineteenth century. Originally a Chinese pagoda, with little roofs flicking up at the edges in ever decreasing tiers, like a Chinese wedding cake, today it appears to be an ancient Gothic ruin, overlooking Swan Pond with its duck-house (q.v.), pheasantry and aviary. As well as monkeys, it has housed swans and boars, and at one time it became an aviary. The Cassillis family would take tea in a little room at the top of the tower, which was once used as a studio.

Culzean is alive with animal buildings: there are also the stately stables, ox-houses, pigsties and cattle-houses of the home farm, the trout hatchery, and the early nineteenth-century hound kennels. In 1945 the Adam house and its estate were given to the National Trust of Scotland by the Fifth Marquess of Ailsa and the Kennedy family, and in 1969 the grounds were declared to be Scotland's first country park.

The pheasantry, poultry-house and aviary were built by Robert Lugar, who affirmed that 'to buildings of the cottage class, or cottage ornée … considerable indulgence should be allowed, and the fastidious should be disarmed of criticism, when the picturesque and the useful should be conveniently and pleasingly united.'

The little house was known as Swan Cottage and was inhabited by the keeper, with the poultry in three rooms on either side, the pheasants in the internal courtyard to the back, and the great quantity of ducks, swans and wild fowl on the lake by which it stands. All was in the best tradition of estate management and of the picturesque. In the cottage the birds were reared for sport and for the kitchen, and in the Gothic aviary for the aesthete and the ornithologist.

Lugar built an identical building as an entrance lodge for the Earl at St Margaret's, Isleworth, in 1811, marking 'the entrance to one of the most beautiful spots on the banks of the River Thames'.

Knole

'That queer little sham Gothic house called the Bird House', wrote Vita Sackville-West in *Knole and the Sackvilles*, 'always frightened me as a child because I thought it looked like a witch's house in *Hansel and Gretel*, tucked away in its hollow with its pointed gables.' It was built *c.* 1761, to house exotic birds, doves and poultry, under the directions of Captain Robert Smith – a parasitic figure who lived for some time at Knole with the Second Duke of Dorset and his wife, 'a very short, very plain, very yellow and vain girl, full of Greek and Latin'. The Duke himself is written of as a mad, disastrous and 'disgusted' figure who would dress up as a Roman emperor, produce operas, and spend vast sums of money defending singers in legal battles. He wrote a large quantity of very bad poetry.

The main door and windows of the bird-house are thought to be genuinely medieval, and to have come from the Archbishop's Palace at Otford, three miles away.

Cardigan Road, Leeds

The bear-pit at Cardigan Road in Leeds is almost all that remains of William Billington and Edward Davis's splendid Zoological and Botanical Gardens, which were opened on 8 July 1840. This little castle, now surrounded by late Victorian villas and squat blocks of flats, and faced by a thundering road, was once part of a great scheme 'for the amusement of the humble classes, which would assist to wean them from debasing pleasures.'

Twenty undulating acres were bought, and classical lodges, conservatories and greenhouses were built. The landscaping was on a grand scale, with gravel walks between the already established trees, surrounded by rare shrubs, flowers and parterres. There were two lakes with islands for water fowl reached by rustic bridges, fountains, statues and winding walls trained with fruit trees. The bears were on display in a round brick-lined pit sunk into the hill behind this façade, viewed either through the portcullis between the turrets or from above when you had climbed the stone stairs in one of the towers. The *Leeds Intelligencier* of 11 July 1840 wrote of the grim attraction of live jackdaws and rooks being let loose in the hawks' cage.

Altogether, it had cost £11,000 and was thought to be the most elegant success. There were bands, concerts, firework displays and exhibitions, all, it was reported, attended by the most 'respectable and influential families in the town'. Sadly, they were not aspiring to their original improving ideals, and the opening boasted an attendance of '2,000 people principally of the higher classes of society'. The grandeur was their downfall. It was thought unnecessary to open every day, and within eight years all had collapsed. The gardens were sold in 1848 to a banker for £6,010. Everything, apart from the outside wall and the bear-pit, was dismantled in 1858.

Penshurst Smithy

The smithy at Penshurst in Kent, now used as a garage, is part of a village built largely in the 1850s as part of George Devy's pioneering plan to consider the local traditions of houses and land-scape. The mock Tudor blacksmith, with its horseshoe doorway, harmonises with the 'Kent vernacular' of the saddlery and the butcher, and at a glance the village appears indigenous to its surroundings.

Gonalston Smithy

The smithy at Gonalston in Nottinghamshire was built entirely of brick, with the 'fullered' (grooved) shoe painted black and the 'nails' painted white. The datestone has the initials of John Francklin of Gonalston Hall, who built and improved several estate cottages in the village, and of course the date of the building, 1843.

There are blacksmiths with great horseshoe doors all over England, embracing you as you enter with the origins of their trade. At Machynlleth in Powys one of stone surrounds the door; there is a shoe round the smithy at Dunmore in Scotland; and at Belton in Lincolnshire a stone horseshoe decorates the Dutch gable above the door.

Ford Blacksmith's Forge

The blacksmith's forge at Ford in Northumberland, in stone like the rest of the village, was built in 1863 by the Marchioness of Waterford, 'a saintly woman, nobly planned ... one of those all accomplished finely-tempered spirits who are rarely seen on this side of paradise; one whom nature has made and then broken the mould.' After her husband's death in 1859, she devoted herself to the building of a model village at Ford, with stone and bargeboarded cottages, a Jubilee Hall and a handsome schoolhouse where, in great biblical murals, she used such models as Jimmy Locke the joiner's son as Jesus, Peter Roule the butcher's boy as David, and Dickie Dunn the head game-keeper as St Paul.

Beatrix Potter, visiting in the 1890s, intensely disliked its perfection: 'No cocks or hens allowed ... a peacock strutting about ... If I had lived there I should have let loose a great parcel of sighs.'

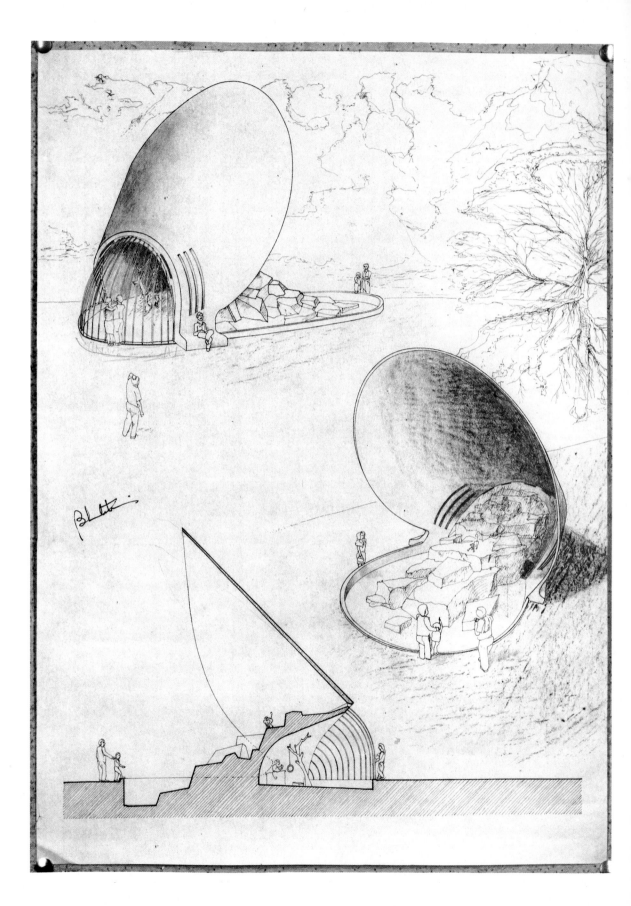

London Zoo

George Scharf's domed and trellised monkey-house (*below*), the first to appear in England, was standing when London Zoo opened its gates to the public in 1829. Five acres of landscaped gardens had been laid out, with 'the added attraction of a delightful promenade' past the creatures in their cages, houses, pools and enclosures. Decimus Burton had designed a macaw cage, the camel-house, a small, heavily bargeboarded building with a clock tower, and the original urned, pedimented and balustraded tunnel, which was found to be too low for an elephant with a howdah. The zebras and mountain-goats sheltered in a Swiss chalet, and everywhere on the skyline there appeared an architectural protruberance – a thatched roof, a spiked finial, a dome, a pediment or a weather-vane.

The Zoological Society's publication of 1830 records that nine species inhabited this handsome monkey-house, including the 'Collared White Eyelid Monkey' and the 'Lesser White-Nosed Monkey', and in 1830 the first orang-utan to come to England was sent to London Zoo. On the journey from Calcutta, the boat stopped for a few days at Mauritius, where he was allowed to go shopping alone every morning for his breakfast. He died within days of arriving in England.

The first chimpanzee arrived at Regent's Park in 1835, and the first gibbons in 1839. That year there was an outbreak of tuberculosis in the cage which struck most of its inhabitants. Although imposing, the monkey-house had always been unhealthily cramped in its living quarters, and a new one was built by 1840.

Lubetkin and Tecton designed a remarkable, but sadly unexecuted, gibbon-house (*left*) for London Zoo. It was said that Julian Huxley, with his overbearing backing of the plan and unwillingness to discuss modifications, turned the zoo directors against it and prevented these strange forms from being built.

Eaton Hall

The parrot-house at Eaton Hall in Cheshire was built by Alfred Waterhouse between 1881 and 1883, when he was working for the First Duke of Westminster, transforming the delicately pinnacled, fairytale palace of William Porden (already slightly altered by William Burn) into a high-Victorian, Gargantua-like palace, which cost £600,000 to build. Now Waterhouse's building has in its turn given way – to the giant concrete bungalow (it is in fact on three floors, but the word describes it perfectly) by John Dennys which stands today.

The parrot-house replaced a conservatory which had been built in 1822 at the north end of the 350-foot long main terrace. It faced a Gothic temple housing a Roman altar found by workmen digging nearby. Waterhouse's building is of the palest terracotta and was once topped with a green copper dome, ornamented with vitreous mosaic by one Mr Rust. Griffins, with tails entwined, stand around the frieze above the niches and Doric pilasters, and caryatids in the clerestory support the roof. Beneath the mosaic floor there is a space of about six feet which was filled with pipes heated from a coal boiler behind the building. They warmed water flowing in brick channels beside them, so that it evaporated up through grilles in the floor to create a perfect jungle-like humidity.

Death

Blockley

A memorial to a trout was put up in the gardens at Fish Cottage in Blockley, Gloucestershire, by the son of the man who tamed it: William Keyte, a wheelwright, and judging from the photographs that survive a distinguished Gladstonian figure, in his stove-pipe hat. His son Charles inscribed the tablet to honour the remarkable affection which existed between his father and the fish, which used to rise to the surface whenever the old man went near the pond. The trout died in 1855. It is said that it was murdered.

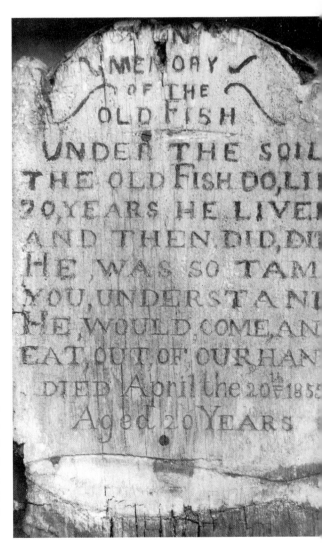

Longworth *(on previous page)*

An exceedingly pretty fluted urn to the memory of a racehorse rests in the grounds of the eight-eenth-century Longworth Hall at Lugwardine in Hereford. It was found in the cellar of the house by the then owner Henry Barneby, in the 1880s. He restored and re-erected it, placing it so that it overlooked the brick-bayed house and the River Frome.

Dunham Massey

There are many eighteenth-century tombstones for dogs (Poor Cato, Tipler, Old Towzer, Old Virtue, Puce, Bijoux and Lyon) in the gardens of Dunham Massey in Cheshire. They would have been put there by the owners of the day: the First Earl of Warrington, the Second Earl, his daughter Lady Stamford, and in turn her son, who revived the name of Warrington. Henry Booth, the First Earl, was tried for treason in 1686 when his friendship with Monmouth had put him in a perilous position. He later rose against James II and was eventually made Chancellor of the Exchequer by William of Orange. The Second Earl's claim to public attention was through his family petitioning Parliament with the claim that he had left them destitute. He hated his wife, and published a paper on the advisability of divorce on the grounds of incompatibility. It was he who rebuilt the Tudor house in the first half of the eighteenth century.

A portrait of Old Virtue by Leonard Knyff in the house, painted *c.* 1697, shows a fat brindled pug in front of the Tudor pile, with a giant swooping swallow and a pastoral scene of deer and leaping sheep. The Booth dogs went on being commemorated well into the nineteenth century, with memorials to Gipsy, Beam, Faithful, Dash, Fop and Marquis.

Farley Mount

The thirty foot pyramid – once rendered grey but recently restored to a brilliant cream – soaring above Hampshire on the Mount at Farley Down was built between 1730 and 1740 to commemorate the bravery and feats of a horse who had jumped safely into a twenty-five foot deep chalk pit come upon unexpectedly while out hunting. His rider, Sir Paulet St John, was saved, and together with his horse, now renamed 'Beware Chalk Pit', went on a year later to win the Hunters' Plate on Worthy Down.

Easton Neston

Elegantly incised letters 'To the Memory of PUG' decorate a stone slab in the garden temple at Easton Neston in Northamptonshire, built in 1641. The slab, at least six inches thick and laid on top of two crudely carved 'legs', looks like a rough stone table, and there seems to be no connection with the creature it commemorates until you spot a pug carved into the swags of the odd supports. Heraldic horses rear up at either end.

Easton Neston, remodelled by Nicholas Hawksmoor in 1702, is thought to be the model for Jane Austen's Mansfield Park. 'Pug', therefore, might well be the model for Lady Bertram's pet dog, 'my poor Pug', her most amiable companion.

Not unlamented now she dies:
Besprinkled here this Tribute lies
With heavenly tears from Angels' Eyes.

Rousham

William Kent was called in by General James Dormer in 1738 to apply his vision of the picturesque to the gardens at Rousham. With weaving and curvaceous planting he was to soften Bridgeman's rather awkward landscaping of the 1720s. Throwing the garden open to the countryside at one turn, and placing a temple or a statue within its folds at every other, he created a perfect embodiment of the picturesque, which has survived intact. There is a great arcade of pedimented arches, a statue of a lion attacking a horse, by Sheemakers, a temple, a grotto, a pyramid house and a Gothic seat/cow-house (q.v.). An eyecatcher and a folly beyond make the countryside part of and, as it were, embraced by the undulating garden.

The cascades in 'Venus Vale', with the statue of Venus above the memorial stone to Ringwood – 'an otter hound of extraordinary sagacity' – were part of a grand plan, with chains of ponds linked to the arches. A strange and narrow stone drain still curves down from them to the River Cherwell:

> Tyrant of the Cherwell's Flood
> Come not near this Sacred Gloom,
> Nor, with thy insulting Brood,
> Dare pollute my Ringwood's Tomb.

Also at Rousham, a stone slab was put up to commemorate Faustina Gwynne, a cow. She and her sister, Goody Gwynne, were short-horns brought from Northamptonshire in 1873. Very brilliant chestnut with white speckles, she was the terror of the village and would chase people down the street at every opportunity. There is a watercolour of her in the house – handsome and huge with a table-flat back. The Cottrell Dormer family still have her horns.

16 Cheyne Walk

In 1862 Dante Gabriel Rossetti, miserable after his wife Elizabeth Siddal's death, moved to 16 Cheyne Walk, where he was to live for the rest of his life. There was almost an acre of garden, allowed to get more overgrown by the day, and in it he kept a menagerie which became the despair of his neighbours: a cook nearby was startled out of her wits by an armadillo burrowing through the floor of her kitchen; another was enraged by a racoon making off with the eggs.

There were two wombats, a chameleon, a wallaby, a marmot, a jackass, a racoon, a woodchuck, a deer, and salamanders and armadillos, as well as two kangaroos (the mother was killed by her son), peacocks (one had its tail stamped off by the deer), green lizards, Chinese horned owls and many more – with innumerable little creatures such as dormice, hedgehogs and a mole. Rossetti bought a Brahmin bull; gossip said he likened its eyes to those of William Morris's wife, Janey. After charging through the house and out into the garden on the first day, it charged back through the house and out into the street on the second, pursuing Rossetti at speed. He tried to buy an elephant to clean the windows. It was an excellent plan: people would stop to ask who lived there and go in to buy his pictures.

The wombats were his favourites. He was in Scotland when they arrived, but was moved to a pitch of anticipatory excitement:

> Oh, how the family affections combat
> Within this heart, and each hour flings a
> bomb at
> My burning soul! Neither from owl nor from
> bat
> Can peace be gained until I clasp my wombat.

They spent much of the time in the house sleeping in hanging lamps and being nursed by Rossetti. Mrs Virtue Tebbs, a solicitor's wife who was sitting for Rossetti, was less charmed. The wombats ate her straw hat. 'Oh poor wombat! It is so indigestible!' wailed Rossetti.

I never reared a young Wombat
To glad me with his pin-hole eye,
But when he most was sweet & fat
And tail-less, he was sure to die!

Brockelesby

There is a monument to the memory of Dashaway, the Earl of Yarborough's favourite hunter of the 1880s, at Brockelesby. Lord Yarborough loved this horse, and had him painted in 1892 by Evans. The great picture hangs in the passage that connects the house to the stables (q.v.).

Newstead Abbey

Boatswain, Lord Byron's Newfoundland, died of rabies at Newstead Abbey in 1808. Byron thought his monument to the dog was set exactly on the site of the high altar of the church of the old abbey, but modern scholarship judges the urn to be in the middle of the east wall. There are three vaults beneath the monument, and in his will of 1811 Byron wrote that he wished to be buried in one of them, beside his dog and his manservant. When Boatswain was dying, Byron, according to Thomas Moore, was 'so little aware … of the nature of the malady that he, more than once, with his bare hand, wiped away the saliva from the dog's lips during the paroxysms.'

The inscription to Boatswain describes him as possessing:

Beauty without Vanity
Strength without Insolence
Courage without Ferocity
and all the Virtues of Man without his Vices.

Byron had surrounded himself with animals from his days at Cambridge, where he had kept a bear. In Italy he had a menagerie, with two monkeys, peahens, nine horses, a goat, several dogs and three geese, who were allowed to wander at will. Lady Byron had a cynical view of her husband's love for animals: 'Reason why some tyrannical characters have been fond of animals – and humane to them – because they had no EXERCISE OF REASON, and could not condemn the wickedness of their Master.'

Wynyard Park

The tombstones and monuments to Lady Londonderry's dogs, with inscriptions by Henry Liddell (Lord Ravensworth), are elegantly placed in a parkscape of exceptional beauty at Wynyard Park in County Durham. Frances Anne, Marchioness of Londonderry, was known as the grandest hostess in England. She sailed through society in 'the family fender' (an enormous tiara), entertaining such figures as Sir Thomas Lawrence, Sir Robert Peel, Prince Louis Napoleon, Sir Walter Scott and the Duke of Wellington. Disraeli, arriving at Wynyard one day, said that never in his life had he anticipated such happiness, and in

1832 Thomas Rose wrote of its charms: 'The Walls and pleasure grounds in the vicinage of the edifice harmonise well with the chaste design of the architect; artificial decoration and superb ornament, give place to softer features of nature. A small rivulet, forming a beautiful canal margined with wood and shady walks, meanders with easy curvatures through the park and gives a delightful finish to the scene.'

The tombs are well cared for, and the present Lord Londonderry has added some of his own, including a stone slab laid in a bower of beeches with a verse written in 1964 to his bulldog Butch.

Southill

The drinking-trough monument to Lady Elizabeth Whitbread's spaniel Jock at Southill was commissioned by Samuel Whitbread, the son of the founder of the brewery; he also wrote the commemorative verse:

> Ye dogs who in succession share
> Your kindest lady's tender care
> Drink at this fount, for see above
> A model of the truest love
> That ever warmed your faithful race.

He asked George Gerrard, the sculptor and painter of animals, to sculpt this elegant little dog on its elegant little Coade stone pedestal. Gerrard also produced a delightful array of plaster creatures to decorate the rooms of the eighteenth-century house. In the old hall, lions, bulls, deer, horses and, unexpectedly, bison and camels peer down from above the doors. Gerrard was initially a painter, turning to sculpture when he thought how useful it would be for his fellow artists were he to model such animals as cattle and sheep for them to paint into their landscapes. He exhibited 215 times at the Royal Academy, and was responsible in 1798 for the passing of the Act of Parliament which enabled sculptors to secure copyright in their works.

Woburn

The temple to a pekinese, Che Foo, at Woburn Abbey in Bedfordshire was built by the 'Flying Duchess of Bedford', so called for her spirited achievement in having learned to fly at sixty-one; she made a record flight to India three years later.

A bronze effigy of the dog by P. V. de Kerckhovey lives on the plinth. Both his dynastic and his familiar names, Che Foo and Wuzzy, are inscribed below, with the dates of his birth (December 1904) and death (28 July 1916), and part of a verse by Byron:

> In life the firmest friend,
> The first to welcome, foremost to defend.

The memorial has a stepped circular base. Six Corinthian columns with carved decorative bands encircle the tomb, linked by benches, each supported by a lion's foot. A stone frieze of swags and fruit carries the wrought-iron dome. The temple is about twelve feet high and stands alone in a copse, some distance from the house.

When her pekinese died, the Duchess made a desolate entry in her diary: 'My little Che Foo died. He has been my constant companion for over eleven years and a more faithful and devoted one I shall never have.'

Wimborne St Giles

In 1887, the newly widowed daughter-in-law of the Seventh Earl of Shaftesbury, the great philanthropist, called in the architect G. F. Bodley to Gothicise the Georgian church of St Giles at Wimborne St Giles in Dorset. In the midst of the work, with the building open to the skies, two robins nested south of the high altar. All activity around them was stopped immediately, and for weeks the workmen took care not to disturb the birds, taking up their work again only when the fledglings had flown. The robin, with the blood of Christ on his breast where he plucked from the crown of thorns on the road to Calvary, had always been thought of as a sacred bird in England, and their nesting in the church was considered a good omen.

The workmen put the nest in a jar, with an account of what had happened, and built it into the wall. Twenty years later, in 1908, after a fire, the architect Sir Ninian Cowper, pupil of Bodley, was commissioned to repair the damage and make various alterations of his own. Once again two robins nested, in the same area south of the high altar; once again they were left undisturbed; and once again it was decided to build the nest into the church. They found the first nest when they were concealing the second, having known nothing of what had gone on before.

His Master's Voice

The plaque to mark the burial place of Nipper, the fox/bull-terrier of 'His Master's Voice', originally in a luxuriant garden with the mulberry tree beneath which he was buried in 1895, is now in the car park of Lloyds Bank, Clarence Street, Kingston-upon-Thames. It was Francis Barrand who originally painted Nipper, three years after the dog's death, staring into the horn of a cylinder phonograph. He worked from a photograph. The 'Gramophone Company' wanted to buy it, but only if Nipper could appear entranced with one of their own machines. Barrand was paid £100, £50 for the copyright, £50 for the painting. 'Nipper was a really clever little dog – of course one is always inclined to think one's own dog cleverer than those belonging to other people – but he was most original', wrote Barrand. His nipping and ebullient character was one to be teased, and Barrand would often give him soda-water which he would battle with, barking louder and louder as his tongue lapped the fizz. He never hesitated to fight with any dog he met, and lost his right eye ratting. In the original photograph he faces the other way, but such a detail had of course to be hidden in the painting. When there is a fire drill at Thorn/EMI at Hayes in Middlesex, the firemen are told to save the painting before anything else.

Toby is the dog in this photograph. He was chosen from 150 as looking most like Nipper, and tours the land promoting the memory of his famous predecessor.

Ilford Pet Cemetery

Ilford Pet Cemetery, a last resting place for a rabbit, a tortoise, a canary, a parrot and a budgerigar, is full of tombs to war heroes. During the Second World War, dogs were trained to sniff out mines and ammunition, bear messages through the firing line, warn of air-raids and, on patrol, of the approaching enemy, and nose out and rescue victims in the rubble of a bomb attack. Many of these courageous creatures are buried here, through the archway emblazoned with the words, 'They are ever in our thoughts, love never dies.'

'Beauty' was a wire-haired terrier, the mascot of the PDSA bomb rescue squad who so furiously pursued her duties that she had to be issued with leather boots to protect her raw little feet. She was awarded the Dickin Medal, with its ribbons of blue, brown and green, for valour 'in the sky, on land and on sea', as was 'Antis', an alsatian rescued as a starving puppy by Jan Bozech, a Czech air-gunner shot down over Germany, with whom he was to have the most harrowing adventures of escape. They were shot down over the sea and rescued by the Italian navy, only to be sunk within days by a British warship. Bozech was later to join the RAF, and Antis would sneak secretly onto his flights, twice being horribly wounded. Until the end of the war, he distinguished himself with the bomb rescue squad and was often to warn his master of approaching aircraft. They returned together to Czechoslovakia after 1945, but Bozech soon fell foul of the authorities, and another escape was embarked upon. Twice he was saved from death by the dog.

The pigeon too played a heroic role in the war. Two hundred thousand birds were used, and as they could fly a mile a minute they were able time and again to save lives by locating the position of the enemy, their ammunition sites, a shot-down aircraft or a stranded platoon. 'Mary of Exeter', buried at Ilford, was one of the bravest. She worked for five years and, often seriously wounded, would limp home riddled with bullets. She had twenty-two stitches in her tiny body. On 29 November 1945 she also was presented with the Dickin Medal.

ANTIS D.M.
ALSATIAN

DIED 11TH AUGUST 1953,
AGED 14 YEARS

THERE IS AN OLD BELIEF
THAT ON SOME SOLEMN SHORE,
BEYOND THE SPHERE OF GRIEF,
DEAR FRIENDS SHALL MEET ONCE MORE.

VERNY AŽ DO SMRTI

MEMORY OF EXETER
AWARDED DICKIN MEDAL
1940

Memory of
TORTY
PET OF THE FAMILY
DIED 12 SEPT 1963
AGED 10 YEARS.

30.

Crawshawbooth

Rossendale Pets Memorial Gardens at Crawshawbooth in Lancashire is gleamingly neat, bright and clean, in startling contrast to the grim surrounding landscape. In the late 1960s, a farmer ran over his dog with a tractor, buried it, and thus started this 1,000-plot cemetery. There are six ponies, two monkeys, rabbits, budgerigars, cats and dogs under marble and granite tombs. Rossendale has on average one funeral a week, with the corpse laid out in a 'lovely polished wood casket with an inscribed plate.' A condition of burial is that the planting is entirely the responsibility of Mr Holt, the owner, who every year beds out some 17,000 plants in June and adds to the mass of bulbs in the autumn.

So shocked was Mr Holt by the practices of the skin trade with domestic pets, which was rampant in Lancashire and Yorkshire, that he opened the more modestly priced crematorium, in which the names are incised on small Westmorland green slate plaques among the 243 plots. It is part of the veterinary service that your pet is cremated, but at Rossendale their ashes are scattered on the Garden of Remembrance and your slate plaque is placed either in the Wall of Remembrance or on the ground.

Fairford

A monument to 'Tiddles the Church Cat, 1963–1980', can be found sitting among the distinguished seventeenth- and eighteenth-century tombs of St Mary the Virgin at Fairford in Gloucestershire. She was a tabby cat who lived in the church, summer and winter, for fifteen years, welcoming visitors and sitting on the congregation's knees during the service. Hating the company of a labrador puppy, she had left home one day and gone to the church. Mr Sidney Jacques, the verger ('She ruled you', insisted Mrs Jacques), fed and looked after her, and when she died he buried her, commissioning Peter Juggins to carve her likeness in the churchyard. 'She spent more time in the church than anyone else and deserved a plot of her own.'

Henley

JIMMY
A TINY MARMOSET
AUGUST 16th 1937
THERE ISN'T ENOUGH
DARKNESS IN THE WORLD
TO QUENCH THE LIGHT
OF ONE SMALL CANDLE

Quite by chance, in May 1983, an old gentleman was walking past this gravestone, which stands on the edge of the main Henley to Oxford road, who remembered this little marmoset. He used to be wrapped around his mistress's neck like a fox fur, and whenever anyone attempted to stroke him he would gnash out with a vicious and painful bite.

Shugborough

There are two very different theories about the life of this nobly elevated cat on its eighteenth-century plinth. One is that it circumnavigated the world with Admiral Lord Anson, who made his five-year journey around the world, from 1740 to 1744, in the flagship *Centurion*. They took three months to round Cape Horn, saved Canton from being burned to the ground, and captured a galleon worth £400,000. In keeping with tradition, there was a ship's cat, and it is said that this monument was the Admiral's tribute ... except that the plaque is made of artificial stone of a much later date, the late 1760s, by which time Lord Anson was dead and the cat would have reached the age of at least thirty.

The second theory is that the plinth was erected by Thomas Anson, the Admiral's elder brother, who inherited Shugborough and transformed it to a vision of the picturesque, building a Chinese house designed from drawings of Canton done by an officer on the *Centurion*, and a quantity of temples, arches, bridges, 'ruins' and monuments. The cat may have been another – built to honour a pet, or perhaps several, as Thomas Anson is recorded to have had many that died from distemper.

Mount Edgcumbe

An obelisk to a pig stands high on a hilltop overlooking Plymouth. Stately, substantial and some thirty feet high, it was put up in the second half of the eighteenth century by the Countess of Mount Edgcumbe to her pet pig Cupid, her most faithful companion. Cupid would follow her about wherever she went, coming in to meals and even going with her on visits to London. When he died, according to a local paper, he was 'buried in a gold casket, the spot being marked by the obelisk on the instruction of the Countess.' Her grief was satirised by Dr John Walcot, who versified under the name of Peter Pinder:

> O dry that tear so round and big,
> Nor waste in sighs your precious wind,
> Death only takes a single pig –
> Your Lord and son are left behind.

Walcot also writes of George III standing pondering near the grave when he visited Mount Edgcumbe in 1789: 'The Queen from a distance asked him what he was looking at. The King with ready humour replied: "The family vault, Charly, family vault, family vault".'

The obelisk was moved from the grounds of Mount Edgcumbe in the 1860s to stand on the prominence overlooking the Sound where the River Tamar joins the English Channel.

Prickle's Monument

The design for a monument to Prickle, a much loved dog who died on 13 December 1984, will stand at the bottom of the garden of the Old Rectory, Hedgerley, in Buckinghamshire. Nine and a half feet high, four feet wide, and two feet deep, it will be cast in reconstituted Bath stone, in a series of twelve moulds, with soaring crockets and pinnacles in sympathy with her name. Four gargoyles of canine weepers will be cast in a bronze-finished resin. The design is by Alan Dodd, inspired by the tomb of St Peter Martyr at S. Eustorgio, Milan.

Prickle, cast in the bronzed resin, will sit on a tasselled cushion, prepared to face her master on the day of judgement. She was bought in 1964 at Shepherd's Bush market for 10s, and never was any money better spent.

Bibliography

P. Toynbee, ed., *Horace Walpole's Journals of Visits to Country Seats* (1763)

W. Hutchinson, *The History of Cumberland* (1794)

F. Elrington Bell, *History of the County of Dublin*, ii (Alex Thom, 1803)

H. Repton, *Designs for the Pavilions at Brighton* (1808)

J. Nichols, *Literary Anecdotes of the Eighteenth Century* (1815)

J. Nichols, *The Progresses and Public Processions of Queen Elizabeth* (1823)

—— *The Gardens and Menagerie of the Zoological Society Delineated: Quadrupeds* (Royal Zoological Society, 1830)

Prince Pückler Muskau, *Tour in England, Ireland and France in the Years 1828 and 1829*, 4 vols (Effingham Wilson, 1832)

J. C. Loudon, *The Encyclopaedia of Cottage, Farm and Villa Architecture* (1833)

Sir N. W. Wraxall, Bt, *Posthumous Memoirs of His Own Time* (Richard Bently, 1836)

I. Eller, *The History of Belvoir Castle* (R. Tyas & R. Groombridge, 1841)

E. Burritt, *London to Land's End* (Simpson Low, 1865)

H. Lonsdale, *The Worthies of Cumberland* (George Routledge, 1872)

W. Cobbett, *Rural Rides*, i–ii (Reeves & Turner, 1885)

F. J. Furnivall, ed., *Robert Laneham's Letter of 1575* (Shakespeare Society, 1890)

J. J. Hissey, *Across England in a Dog Cart* (Richard Bently, 1891)

T. F. Dale, *The History of the Belvoir Hunt* (Constable, 1899)

I. Walton, *The Compleat Angler* (Bodley Head, 1904)

A. O. Cooke, *A Book of Dovecotes* (T. N. Foulis, 1920)

W. Bingham Compton, Sixth Marquis of Northampton, *History of the Comptons of Compton Wynyates* (Bodley Head, 1930)

D. Smith, *Pigeoncotes and Dovecotes of Essex* (Simpkin Marshall, 1931)

R. Kipling, *Collected Dog Stories* (Macmillan, 1934)

—— *Men, Women and Things: Memoirs of the Duke of Portland* (Faber & Faber, 1937)

V. Sackville-West, *Knole and the Sackvilles* (W. Heinemann, 1934)

A. S. Turberville, *A History of Welbeck and its Owners*, ii (Faber & Faber, 1939)

W. Gaunt, *The Pre-Raphaelite Dream* (Jonathan Cape/The Reprint Society, 1943)

M. S. Briggs, *The English Farmhouse* (Batsford, 1953)

B. Jones, *Follies and Grottoes* (Constable, 1953)

D. Stroud, *The Architect John Soane* (Studio Books, 1961)

G. Pedrick, *Life with Rossetti* (Macdonald, 1964)

E. S. Turner, *All Heaven in a Rage* (Michael Joseph, 1964)

J. B. Priestley, *The Prince of Pleasure* (Heinemann, 1969)

M. Girouard, *The Victorian Country House* (Clarendon Press, Oxford, 1971)

D. Guinness and W. Ryan, *Irish Houses and Castles* (Irish Georgian Society, 1971)

D. Rybot, *It Began Before Noah* (Michael Joseph, 1972)

J. M. Crook and M. H. Port, *History of the King's Works*, vi (HMSO, 1973)

L. Petts, ed., *The Story of Nipper and the His Master's Voice Picture* (The Gramophone Company, 1973)

D. L. Moore, *Accounts Rendered* (John Murray, 1974)

J. Macaulay, *The Gothic Revival: 1745–1845* (Blackie, 1975)

W. Blunt, *The Ark in the Park: The Zoo in the Nineteenth Century* (Hamish Hamilton, 1979)

P. Conner, *Oriental Architecture in the West* (Thames & Hudson, 1979)

J. Summerson, *The Life and Works of John Nash* (Allen & Unwin, 1980)

C. Aslet, *The Last Country Houses* (Yale University Press, 1982)

D. Watkin, *The English Vision* (John Murray, 1982)

H. Hobhouse, *Prince Albert: His Life and Work* (Hamish Hamilton, 1983)

J. M. Robinson, *Georgian Model Farms* (Clarendon Press, Oxford, 1983)

K. Thomas, *Man and the Natural World* (Allen Lane, 1983)

P. Coe and M. Reading, *Lubetkin and Tecton: Architecture and Social Commitment* (Arts Council, 1984)

Index

Tailpiece

Robert Watson, Master of the Carlow Hounds in Ireland, became convinced in later life that he was a fox, and built this handsome, Gothic-entranced 'earth' for himself at Larch Hill in County Meath. He was one of the first men in Ireland to breed foxhounds, and killed the last wolf in the country, leaving a Quaker Meeting to do so. 'He went completely bonkers as far as one can gather', says his great-great-grand-daughter, the distinguished art historian Anne Crookshank.